THE PHILOSOPHER AND THEOLOGY

THE PHILOSOPHER AND THEOLOGY is the philosophical memoirs of one of the greatest living thinkers of our time, Etienne Gilson, who has won worldwide recognition for his zealous defense of intellectual freedom and for his extraordinary erudition. In this autobiographical narrative, Gilson retraces his early education in the Catholic faith and its lasting influence on his life and thought, and describes his educational career at the University of Paris, where the always dynamic interaction of diverse schools of thought led him to his lifelong dedication to philosophical discourse.

Gilson became a scholar of Descartes, and through Descartes and under the brilliant direction of Lévy-Bruhl, while at the Sorbonne he began a deep and unique study of medieval thought, which has resulted in his revolutionizing the understanding of early Christian thought and especially St. Thomas, and has brought to the modern world a new concept of Christian philosophy. In dealing with the main problems of his career as philosopher-scholar, Gilson gives a first-hand account of the attitudes and thoughts of such outstanding men as Durkheim, Brunschvicg, Péguy, Lévy-Bruhl and especially the Jewish philosopher Bergson, whose philosophy has had such an effect on modern Catholic thinkers.

THE PHILOSOPHER AND THEOLOGY is the warm personal account of the development of a modern Scholastic among the conflicts of twentieth-century thought and those men who have played important roles in the history of philosophy.

THE PHILOSOPHER AND THEOLOGY

THE
PHILOSOPHER

AND THEOLOGY

BY ETIENNE GILSON

Translated from the French by Cécile Gilson

Random House   New York

Design by J. J. Suplina

Philosophy is the handmaid of theology.
Of course. (After all, Mary is the handmaid
of the Lord.) But let not the handmaid
quarrel with the mistress, and let not the mistress
carp at the handmaid. A stranger might
come who would rapidly settle the question.

Charles Péguy

CONTENTS

THE
PHILOSOPHER
AND
THEOLOGY

PREFACE

This book is not a history of contemporary Catholic thought in France. Hence the reader is asked to refrain from accounting for a number of omissions on the basis of any rash premises. Some omissions will be easily explained by my failure to grasp the meaning of certain thinkers; it therefore seemed wise to say nothing of what was little understood. Other omissions are to be explained by the fact that certain doctrines, or persons, however much I admire or love them, have played no part (at least, so far as I know) in shaping the very history I am about to retrace.

The subject of this book is the long adventure of a young Frenchman brought up in the Catholic faith who was indebted to the Church for his entire education and to the University of Paris for his philosophical training, who found himself confronted by Clio with the task of discovering the precise nature of theology, and who, after devoting many years of his life to the discussion of this problem, found the answer too late to put it to use.

It should be noted that the very history of this quest is not here at stake. It would be of little interest. There is nothing new to learn from the mere recounting of the moves and countermoves of a historian who strayed in the past and looked at the flow of events from the wrong end. Rather, let these pages bear witness to the author's many uncertainties. Now that he has seen his way out, it is his sincere hope that he will make it easier for others to avoid them.

I wish to express my gratitude to my daughter Cécile Gilson for Englishing the French original of this book. From the very beginning it was understood between us that its English rendering should be free and not necessarily literal. As always, my friend of long standing Professor A. C. Pegis has been of invaluable assistance, and to him I extend our sincere thanks.

5

THEOLOGICAL INFANCY

A man of seventy-five should have many things to say about his past, but when he is invited to do so, if he has lived only as a philosopher, he immediately realizes that he has no past. From the time of his youth one problem has faced him; it continues to do so, and although he may now be more familiar with its data, he is still at grips with it. Watching him from a distance, a historian would easily prove that it is not so, but the philosopher himself knows well enough that all he may have said successively, all the different assertions which, understood to the letter, sometimes appear contradictory, still ring true to him and from some point of view still meet with his approval. A man does not change simply because he tries to solve the same problem over and over again, and especially not if the data include an unknown quantity whose exact value will always escape him.

If he happens to be a Christian, this same man has the impression of living in a kind of inner solitude. It is not that friends are lacking. On the contrary, life has been generous to him in that respect; but while he shared with other men their joys, their sorrows, and the responsibilities of daily life, there was in him another life whose vicissitudes he was the only one to know. It is impossible to describe the profound continuity of this deeper life without betraying it. This is the common lot of philosophers. Inasmuch as he is one with a problem, which he may possibly share with many other men, but whose expression in his own mind is personal and unique, the philosopher feels that he is living a solitary life. He knows he will die in that solitude, surrounded by obstacles set up by his own intelligence and a prisoner of their insuperable necessity. But he who philosophizes as a Christian feels himself still more hopelessly isolated, especially in the middle

7

of this twentieth century and its deeply dechristianized environment. It is trying and, in the long run, discouraging to go against the general trend. No one, I presume, enjoys feeling different, especially when the very meaning of human life is at stake. The recent controversies about the notion of "Christian philosophy" clearly show to what extent it has become alien to most of our contemporaries. He who carelessly announces his intention to philosophize as a Christian is sure to find himself excluded from the society of philosophers. They simply refuse to listen to what he says.

You may say that, after all, if the Christian philosopher finds his situation uncomfortable, he should simply quit philosophizing as a Christian. Most of the great philosophers have contented themselves with philosophizing as mere philosophers, many Christians today still favor the same attitude, and common sense is all for it. This is true, but the advice comes too late for an old man to follow it. Being a Christian, I personally have no choice. No one is born a Christian, but a man born in a Christian family soon becomes one without having been consulted. He is not even aware of what is happening to him. At baptism, the child receives within himself a sacrament whose effects will decide his future in time and eternity. His godfather says the Creed for him and assumes for him obligations whose terms the child does not even understand, but which are no less binding for him. At any rate, the Church considers him bound by them. When she will ask him later on, as she does every year, to "renew" the promises of baptism, the very same promises once made for him by someone else are those he is invited to make all over again. The grown man is free not to renew them, but there is a great difference between not belonging to a Church and explicitly refusing to belong to it. The non-baptized man is a pagan, the baptized man who refuses to honor the promises of baptism separates himself from the Church to the extent that it is possible for him to do so; he is an apostate. True enough, most of those who lose their faith in this way content themselves with drifting away from the Church. They fall into indifference without abjuring faith. But things are not so easy for a philosopher. A day comes when he has only two choices: either to make in his own name the promises once made for him by another, or formally to refuse to subscribe to them. Had I decided on the latter course I do not know what I would think today: but I do know that, in the full awareness of what I am doing and with the inner certainty of making a free choice, I still formally renew today the vows made in my name a few days after my birth. Some will deem it a grace, to others it will look like a disgrace. Whatever may be the case, not only do I accept these promises personally, I do not remember ever having forgotten them.

This fact makes it hard for me to understand how a Christian can ever philosophize as if he were not a Christian. Baptism is a sacrament; it is not in the Christian's power not to have received its grace. Besides, the simplest of prayers addressed to God is a profession of faith in His existence. The life of prayer engages the child in a personal relationship with God, and it never crosses his mind that his prayer could be without an object. The very names "God," "Jesus," "Mary" immediately bring real persons to his imagination. Since he is conversing with them, how could he doubt their existence? The Church sees to it that no Christian, however young, ever utters words that are meaningless to him. The young communicant is not interested in controversies about transubstantiation, but his devotion to the Eucharist goes straight to its true object.

The consecrated host truly is for him the body and blood of our Lord Jesus Christ, true God and true man, hidden to the eyes of the flesh, but present to the eyes of faith under the appearance of bread. His whole religion is given to him at once in this great sacrament, and if he still knows it imperfectly, he is already able to live it perfectly. The child cannot be a Doctor of the Church, but he can be a saint.

Moreover, elementary as it is, the religious teaching given by the catechism is not to be despised. It used to be and, in some cases, it still is a very serious introduction to Holy Scripture and to theology. In the last decade of the nineteenth century catechisms did not underestimate either reason or philosophy, but their main concern was to explain to children the meaning of the Creed. Now the Creed consists of articles that are expressly called "articles of faith" because the truths they formulate came to be known to man through revelation and they were proposed to his assent as objects of faith. It is precisely because it appeals to faith that the teaching of the catechism deserves to be called "theology." It is truly theology because it rests upon the truth of what God Himself has said concerning His nature, our duties toward Him, and our destiny. Whatever philosophy may have to say will come later, and since it will not be permitted to add anything to the articles of faith, any more than to curtail them, it can well be said that in the order of saving truth philosophy will come, not only later, but too late.

Hence the difficulty for a Christian ever to become "a philosopher like the others." This difficulty also accounts for the fact that other philosophers will agree to keep him out of their company. On the part of non-Christians, this is a justifiable action, but it is not so easy to justify it when it comes from men who, though

Christians, prefer to keep their philosophical thinking free from all contact with religion.

This attitude has always appeared to me surprising, not to say incomprehensible. To be sure, there are many philosophical problems that can be asked and solved without any reference to faith in the word of God, but the same is not true of the master problems of metaphysics, natural theology, and ethics. When the mind of a Christian begins to take an interest in metaphysics, the faith of his childhood has already provided him with the true answers to most of these questions. He still may well wonder *how* they are true, but he knows *that* they are true. As to the *how*, Christian philosophers investigate it when they look for a rational justification of all the revealed truths accessible to the natural light of understanding. Only, when they set to work, the game is already over. It is permissible to feel slightly skeptical when a believer pretends to philosophize in freedom from all religious influence. But, after all, how do we know what goes on in the privacy of a man's personal conscience? In any case, speaking for myself, I have never conceived the possibility of a split conscience divided between faith and philosophy. The Creed of the catechism of Paris has held all the key positions that have dominated, since early childhood, my interpretation of the world. What I then believed I still believe. And without in any way confusing it with my faith, whose essence must be kept pure, I know that the philosophy I have today is wholly encompassed within the sphere of my religious belief.

This early theological initiation leaves an enduring mark in the minds of children. In this respect the child resembles poor and ignorant people who, owing to the teaching of the Gospel, find themselves possessed of a comprehensive view of the world more complete than that given by any philosophy. Unbeknownst to him, the child repeats their experience. Let us only recall the Creed of daily prayers, wherein the answers to the most formidable problems are assumed by the faithful without any discussion. There is only one God, Father almighty, Creator of the universe and its last end, especially the end of man who, after being resurrected in the flesh, is called to know God and to share in His beatitude in eternal life. In the light of these primary truths, a short history of the world then relates the consecution of the crucial moments that mark out its divinely appointed course. Miraculous as they are, these events follow one another in time, but their very being communicates with the eternity from which they flow. In the beginning, the Word, Who was with God and Who is God; at the center of this history, the Word again, but this time the Word made flesh, the Mediator, only Son of the Father, conceived of the Holy Ghost, born of the Virgin Mary, Who died on the cross to save us, Who was buried, descended into hell and arose again from the dead. At the end, still and always the Word, but this time coming from heaven to judge the living and the dead. Thus, as He was in the beginning and in the middle of time, Jesus Christ must one day preside over its end. Pending that day, His presence abides in the Holy Catholic Apostolic and Roman Church, the perfect society which lives by grace and is quickened from within by the Holy Ghost.

The impact of a Christian education on the mind of a youth is all the deeper for associating with the type of humanistic education prevalent for so long in French schools. It is on the decline today, but it was still thriving at the beginning of this century, especially in separate schools conducted by priests. Should classical studies ever disappear from France, their last stronghold would be Catholic schools. Latin is the language of the Church. The sorry degradation of the liturgical texts by their translation into a gradually deteriorating vernacular emphasizes the need for the preservation of a sacred language whose very immutability protects the liturgy against the decay of taste. As his education is thus proceeding in keeping with the spirit of his own tradition, the young Christian imperceptibly becomes familiar with a Latin philosophical terminology (almost entirely Greek in its origin) embedded in the formulas of Christian dogmas. Liturgy itself forces this terminology upon his attention and fixes it in his memory, since he not only hears this language but also speaks it and sings it. Liturgical music permeates the meaning of the words so thoroughly that, thirty-odd years later, he will only have to sing the Preface to himself in order to recall the words: *Non in unius singularitate personae, sed in unius Trinitate substantiae . . . et in personis proprietas, et in essentia unitas.* . . . No mind can ascribe a meaning to such formulas without assimilating something of the philosophical notions they convey. In the liturgy itself, such words as substance, essence, singularity, propriety, person, point out directly and primarily only the mysterious truths contained in Christian dogma. The sentences that these words constitute are not philosophical propositions. Still, even though they do not bind it to any particular philosophy, a mind that has become familiar with them early enough in life will never be able to accept a doctrine that would consider them meaningless. The Church invincibly opposes any philosophical change that would oblige her to modify the received formulation of dogma. And in this the Church is right, for any change in words would entail a change in meaning, and propositions that have for centuries stood the test of councils cannot be altered without religious truth itself being put in jeopardy.

Thus, long before he begins studying philosophy proper, the Christian imbibes definite metaphysical notions. The deepening study of the catechism progressively assumes a heavier load of philosophical speculation; under the name of apologetics, it thus becomes a simplified scholasticism. There is no adolescent to whom, whether in a classroom or a church, proofs of the existence of God have not been given. In the same manner, the creation of the world from nothing and the spirituality of the soul have been rationally established for his benefit. This recourse to philosophy in order to make the acceptance of religious truth easier for the understanding is scholastic theology itself.

Apologetics is nothing if it is not theology, and to the extent that advanced catechism becomes apologetics it reaches the level that Saint Thomas Aquinas attained in his theology from the first pages of the *Summa Contra Gentiles*. The young Christian does not know that he is an apprentice in theology, but this is what he has steadily become; and if to this theoretical instruction we add religious formation, the education of piety, and the practice of sacramental life, which turn abstract notions into so many living realities personally known and dearly loved, we shall easily understand that when for the first time philosophy tries to enter such a mind it finds the place already engaged and solidly occupied. This adolescent *knows* almost nothing, but he firmly *believes* a great many things. Moreover, his mind is accustomed to moving freely from belief to rational knowledge and from knowledge to belief with no other intention than to observe their spontaneous agreement and to probe more deeply into their wondrous harmony. The grating notes caused by the intrusion of philosophies foreign or hostile to the Christian faith are at once eliminated, and in one way or another the dissonances are resolved. Whatever philosophy our young Christian will be taught, if it is truly a pure philosophy wholly unrelated to religious faith, he will be, if not shocked, at least surprised. The cause of his surprise does not necessarily concern any differences in the conclusions, but rather in the state of mind that such a philosophy presupposes. Even if there is perfect agreement between his religious faith and this philosophy, a body of propositions that he had hitherto held as true on the strength of his faith in the word of God is now proposed to him as so many purely rational demonstrations. To take the risk of thus substituting reason for faith, the Church must place a great trust in reason! She does so, however, and she does so with open eyes, but not without exercising prudent foresight.

I was fortunate in learning my religion from priests whose teaching kept me out of trouble when, at the age of eighteen, I had to pass from advanced catechism to straight philosophy. The easy way in which this transition was effected would be more understandable had I learned philosophy under a priest. But such was not the case. I had been a pupil at the Petit Séminaire Notre-Dame-des-Champs, a diocesan high school equally open to future laymen and to future priests. I owe everything to these admirable priests—my religious faith, my passionate love of letters and history, and even my familiarity with music, which is characteristic of all young choir boys. Notre-Dame-des-Champs no longer exists. A thoroughfare now passes where it used to be. Those who advocate a state monopoly in education do not realize the extent of the loss their country would suffer if this came to pass. I shall not describe here the kind of school Notre-Dame-des-Champs was, nor plead once more the cause of separate schools. Their adversaries know full well what they want. They want to eliminate, along with others, the special kind of Frenchmen that Catholic schools are producing. What France may have to gain by such a step, I do not know. I want to say only that, knowing what I owe Catholic schools, were I today to side with their enemies, I would completely despise myself.

It was during my last year of high school that I made up my mind about what my future would be. I had no religious problems, far from it, but I did not feel called to the priesthood. In trying to find out what I would do, I began by asking myself what profession would leave me more intellectual freedom and longer vacations, and since teaching seemed to be the most promising in that respect, I decided to become a teacher. Besides, I felt quite happy in school, and heedlessly mistaking the lot of a pupil who had a good teacher with that of a teacher who had twenty poor pupils, I was dreaming of the pleasant life of a perpetual student who was equally pleased, as I then was, when summer vacation began and when it ended. What should I teach? The humanities, of course, especially French literature, in which I found such an inexhaustible source of joy. It seemed impossible to me that anything else could ever take its place in my mind. Where should I teach? In a state-controlled high school, since, in France, this was practically the only place in which a layman could earn a living as a teacher. The salary was a meager one, to be sure, but it seemed to me then that the man who would not be satisfied with it was not worthy of such a life. Still, I thought it unwise to embark on the career of a non-Catholic high school teacher without ever having seen the inside of at least one such school. This is why, with the full approval of my parents and my teachers, I left Notre-Dame-des-Champs and went to study philosophy at the Lycée Henri-IV.

I have never been sorry that I made this decision, except that to this day I do not know exactly what philosophy they would have taught me at Notre-Dame-des-Champs. However, I can say this much with certainty: it would not have been the philosophy of Saint Thomas Aquinas or even any form of scholasticism. Those who think otherwise are mistaken. The professor of philosophy at Notre-Dame-des-Champs was the Abbé Ehlinger; at the Lycée Henri-IV, it was M. Dereux. But, apart from the fact that one taught in a cassock and the other in a jacket, they both said just about the same things. Had an exchange of professors taken place between the two institutions, the direction of French philosophy would have remained the same. The two professors were preparing their pupils for the same B.A. degree in philosophy and they were doing it in the same way. Both of them taught a mild form of a spiritualism that Victor Cousin himself would not have disowned. The "unifying function of reason" was good M. Dereux' motto; he probably taught me something more, but I have forgotten it.

I understood nothing of philosophy and I realized it. No scholastic successes could convince me to the contrary. Since I felt annoyed at my failure, the following year, while I was doing my military service, I undertook to read two books which seemed to me well suited to help me measure my aptitude in philosophy. These were the *Metaphysical Meditations* by Descartes and the *Introduction to the Life of the Spirit* by Léon Brunschvicg. My obstinate effort and my persistence in reading and rereading them did not bring me the desired enlightenment. The main result of this experience was the increasing awareness of an amazingly gratuitous arbitrariness. This explained why I could not understand what philosophy was about. I understood well enough the meaning of each and every particular sentence, but I failed to grasp the ultimate purpose of the discourse. Unawares, I was already plagued with the incurable metaphysical disease they call *chosisme*, that is, crass realism. Today there is no intellectual infirmity more utterly despised, but I know well enough that one cannot get rid of it. A person like myself who suffers from this ailment speaks only about "things" or about propositions related to things. I was as nonplused by my first contact with idealism as I was later to be by my first encounter with the so-called philosophies of the mind.

Strangely enough, the feeling of annoyance generated by this experience prompted me to pursue it. I reacted to my failure as to a challenge, for at no moment did I think that the responsibility was not entirely mine. Besides, I had reason to expect more of philosophy. I loved Pascal and I knew whole pages of his *Pensées* by heart. True enough, Pascal was known to me as an author in literature, and it was as such that I had learned to admire him. But Pascal was also a philosopher, though I always found him writing, not about notions or "ideas," like Descartes, but about real objects, things, actually existing beings. No one was less inclined "to think about thinking." It was in this direction, as I believed, that one should look to avoid despairing of philosophy. So I gave up the dream of a life devoted to the study and teaching of the humanities. I did it not without regret, but without remorse, and I went to study philosophy at the Faculty of Letters in the University of Paris. The Sorbonne, I thought, was the only place where I was likely to find it.

18

THE WORLD OF SECULAR LEARNING

In 1905 a student who went from a Catholic school to the Sorbonne felt neither embarrassed nor bewildered. It was a different world, but he was prepared for it. He had been brought up to respect the masters of high learning who would one day become his own masters, and he approached them trustingly, eager to put himself under their guidance. There was, however, one reservation. The philosopher-apprentice who was entering this new discipline at the university level did not expect from it any revelation as to what he should think and believe. This had already been settled in his mind; what he wanted was to probe his own thinking and to go to the root of his faith, a double task to be pursued from then on in the midst of indifferent or hostile surroundings. To grow, if possible, in order to survive —this was henceforth his goal and he had to reach it alone, under his own responsibility.

Myths have grown up around the New Sorbonne of the first years of the twentieth century. For those who were fortunate to receive its teaching, none of the so-called crises that supposedly plagued it perceptibly affected their peace of mind. These tales are the work of great newspaper reporters looking for interesting stories. There was some reality at the bottom of their reports, but it had to be enriched with many trimmings in order to turn it into something the public would buy. Charles Péguy, whom we admired so much, in those days wrote accounts that surprised me. Since I found myself in the middle of the spiritual dramas that he described with such gusto, I should have been a privileged spectator, almost an actor, and I looked around to see them, but in vain.

The trouble with these myths is that, by obstructing the view, they prevent the historians from seeing realities that are much more interesting. This is the case with the Durkheim myth. This extraordinary man occupied in 1905 a place apart among the professors of philosophy at the Sorbonne. He himself was a philosopher brought up in the regular French tradition and was just as able as his colleagues to discuss a metaphysical problem in the accepted academic style. He knew the traditional philosophy very well, but he wanted to do away with it. Stern of countenance, with unwavering eyes and an impressive authority of speech, Durkheim felt himself entrusted with the mission of bringing to the condition of a positive science the sociology that Comte imagined he had not only founded but completed. Durkheim knew very well what he wanted, and so did his pupils. For those among us who decided to take up sociology, there was practically no other choice than to accept without reservation the rules of the sociological method laid down by Durkheim. Before being admitted to work within his group, one had to submit to strict questioning in which the master checked the scientific orthodoxy of the candidate as a future sociologist. That was the situation, but no one was obliged to become a sociologist. None of us was ever forced to join the group and none that I can remember ever suffered because he failed to do so. French universities have never been invaded by Durkheimism. The sociological terror so vividly described by Péguy, of which Durkheim would have been the Robespierre, existed only in Péguy's poetic imagination.

Péguy never wrote anything more brilliant than the posthumous fragment, *L'esprit de système*. Written in 1905, this essay is exactly contemporary with the first of the three years during which I studied under Durkheim at the Sorbonne. Despite my admiration for Péguy and my utter disagreement with Durkheim's doctrine, I find myself unable to believe that the brilliant pamphlet of Péguy really deals with the same man I knew. I never saw the sociologist such as the poet depicts him, anxious "to dominate France by dominating Paris, and in dominating Paris to dominate the world." Still less do I see Durkheim, as Péguy describes him, doubting himself, having entirely lost faith in his own doctrine, fearful, literally panic-stricken before the imminent threat of universal bankruptcy, and paying whatever price was necessary in order to delay its coming.

One would like to quote, for the sheer pleasure of doing so, the dramatic narrative of Durkheim's sociological terror modeled by Péguy after the French Revolution. "Blood, blood everywhere, always more blood and always more victims. After Descartes, Kant; after Kant, Bergson; before Bergson, Epictetus, and of all these beheadings nothing remained, nothing save the urge to behead again. Who will ever stop? Blood calls for blood. Death calls for death. In this perpetual outbidding, he who stops is lost." At least Péguy himself does not stop. One cannot read without believing the pages in which the poet relates with visionary precision how the victims of Durkheim went to their death. The Stoics "with stern pride and a serenity of older times"; the Cartesians, like noblemen of the French seventeenth century; the Kantians walking under the infinite urge of absolute duty; finally, the Bergsonians, these youngest of the philosophical family, all died "with incomparable ease; supremely intelligent, keener than most, they had perfectly understood how their own death fitted into the pattern of these events." And, indeed, as true disciples of their master, the Bergsonians alone had seen through sociology and had understood as a fraud what was a fraud: "They had not said one word against the regime, and yet on the small square behind the statue of Claude Bernard, at the top of the stairs leading to the Collège de France, all had known that the regime was dead."

What a man! How can an old Bergsonian read this account today without feeling surprised that he survived the slaughter? But if he consults his own memory, he looks in vain for the name of one of those sheep butchered for their belief in the Bergsonian creed. It would be easier to find the names of martyrs of the Durkheimian cause, for it had enemies as well as friends. The fierce opposition raised at the time by the representatives of conventional history has not helped the career of many a young sociologist. Metaphysicians naturally detested a science that claimed for itself all the functions they had traditionally fulfilled, including the teaching of ethics and religion. Durkheim certainly was dogmatic in his own field, but, as philosophers worthy of the name normally are, he was ready to submit himself to the exigencies of truth such as he found it. No doubt it is only *their* truth, but how could they see a difference between it and *the* truth?

The importance of Durkheimism lies elsewhere. Long before Durkheim, Comte had founded a sociology of an entirely different inspiration. To him, the discovery of this new science marked the culmination of the long history of the positive spirit. Nothing could be more Greek in inspiration than the positive philosophy of this new Aristotle, in which the will to rational intelligibility, present to the human mind from its very origin, reveals itself first by leading the theological spirit from fetishism to monotheism, then by giving rise to the metaphysical spirit, which substitutes causes for gods, and finally to the positivist spirit, whose conquests extend to sociological facts, thereby bringing to completion the classification of the sciences and laying the foundations of a universal society coextensive with the whole of mankind. Comte's sociology is primarily a theory of knowledge. One still breathes in it the air of Athens; in the last analysis, everything in it is accounted for by reasons of which reason itself is ultimately the judge.

Not so with Durkheim, according to whom social facts are first conceived as *things*. The word "things" has been bitterly reproached to him, but I believe unjustly, for in using it Durkheim merely wanted to stress that there are social *facts*. This meant to him that what he used to call "*the* social" shared in the objective solidity of whatever is given in reality as an entity independent of an observer. The reality of social facts is known by the property they have of exercising a *constraint* on the member of any human society. In its turn, the reality of this constraint is evidenced by the fact that any attempt to evade it is attended by a sanction. The punishment can be a diffuse sanction, such as the censure of public opinion, or it can be a concrete and material one, such as a jail sentence, torture, or death, but there always is one. Durkheim had put his finger on one of those elementary evidences that are visible to all, but which no one notices. Discoveries of this sort are the most beautiful of all, and whatever one may think of the doctrine of Durkheim, there is no denying that it is founded in reality.

It is a pity that Durkheim did not make a sociological study of his own sociology. If the doctrine is true, it is itself a sociological fact. A little reflection is enough to reveal its origin and its spirit. The doctrine of Durkheim is a sociology of Leviticus (19:19): "Keep ye my laws. Thou shalt not make thy cattle to gender with beasts of another kind. Thou shalt not sow thy field with different seeds. Thou shalt not wear a garment

that is woven of two sorts." Thus no hybrids, no wool
and cotton cardigans, no wool and silk fabric. Why?
No one knows, except that it is prohibited. "Nor shall
you cut your hair roundwise, nor shave your beard"
(Levit. 19:27–8). The reason is the same: "I am the
Lord." And, no doubt, the reason is good. But let us
notice that a man brought up in a religion in which
prescriptions, interdictions, and sanctions play such an
important part, will naturally tend to conceive "the
social" as a system of restraints imposed from the outside and enforced by sanctions. That these restraints
can sometimes be rationally justifiable is not really
very important; for if they are not thus justifiable, their
authority has in no way diminished. "Of birds these
are they which you must not eat, and which are to be
avoided by you. The eagle, and the griffon, and the
osprey" (Levit. 11:13). Hence, we shall not eat these
birds lest we become unclean and have to be restored
to cleanness. And that is all.

These remarks are in no way meant to be critical. A
metaphysics of being is no less true because it derives
its inspiration from Exodus. Why, then, should not a
sociology be inspired by Leviticus? My only point is
that such a teaching is not more free from all religious
influence, nor is it in any way more purely "rational,"
than the conception of ethics defended by Christian
theologians. There are whole generations of rabbis behind the sociology of Durkheim. In a sense, it is a
Jewish sociology. A Jew brought up in the religion of
his fathers cannot be ignorant of the constraining character of the Law. He cannot be unaware of the burden
that religious observances impose on his life as well as
on the life of his family. I am very far from reproaching
such a sociology with its religious inspiration. What I
am saying is that it should not present itself as a gen-

uine product of the pure speculative reason. Supposing there be any such products, this is not one of them.

All social facts are not listed in Leviticus, but the precepts, commandments, and interdictions of Leviticus certainly are social facts in the sense in which Durkheim understood them. It is therefore easy to see why a philosopher seeking a definition of the "social" as such was first struck by the compulsory nature of the Law to which he himself had been submitted, and to which others around him possibly were still subject. None of this is demonstrable, but it is worthy of remark that the prophet of Durkheimian sociology, Marcel Mauss, belonged to the same ethnic group as the founder of the school. Without Mauss the *Année sociologique* would not have been possible. In any case, his Durkheimian orthodoxy was perfect, uncompromising, almost fierce. One day, in the courtyard of the Sorbonne, some young men were praising him for speaking of religion with true sociological objectivity. Mauss amiably answered: " 'Tis true, I do not attack religion, I dissolve it."

Two swallows do not make spring, but here is a third one. The wonderfully intelligent Lucien Lévy-Bruhl also was a sociologist of note. We owe him the almost incredible book *La morale et la science des moeurs* (1903), in which he calmly stated that to the question, "What should one do?" there was no answer. The major part of his work, however, consisted of a series of studies on the mental activity of inferior societies, in which he described with penetration what he had long called "pre-logical mentality." Toward the end of his life the expression ceased to please him, and this great and honest man said so; but we would be mistaken if we thought that his work became obsolete in the process. Once the formula was discarded, the

bulk of the observations and their analyses still remained. Lucien Lévy-Bruhl subscribed, freely but
wholeheartedly, to the Durkheimian notion of the social
fact conceived as a "given" that obeys laws and can be
scientifically interpreted. A close friendship united him
to Durkheim and even to Mauss, the very same Mauss
of whom Péguy sometimes would make fun: "That
elegance of Mauss, that fine high-German speech. . . ."
The high-German accent of Mauss? Another of those
traits that entirely escaped me and of which I find no
trace in my memory. I did notice, however, that of this
sociological trinity, Lucien Lévy-Bruhl alone enjoyed
an almost miraculous immunity against Péguy's attacks. It must be noted that Péguy himself had been his
pupil before me and kept a grateful affection for him.
Still, when all is said, the fact is that if the sociology of
Durkheim and Mauss was hateful to him, Péguy should
have hated that of Lévy-Bruhl just as much, for it was
the same. As I pointed this out to him one day, Lévy-
Bruhl answered me with a smile: "But this is quite
simple really. *I am a subscriber.*" Then he added softly:
"At the *Cahiers de la Quinzaine,* the subscriber is
sacred."

These names describe a group whose origins some
historian will no doubt one day study. To Durkheim,
Lévy-Bruhl, and Mauss, let us add the name of Rauh.
A high forehead over fiery eyes, a face marked by the
intensity of his thought, Rauh had the voice of a moralist anguished by one single problem: how to found
moral obligation objectively. I studied under him for
two years. The first year he announced that before
undertaking to build (*pars construens*) one should first
destroy (*pars destruens*). Rightly or wrongly, I had
imagined that all the wreckage would be done in a
year, but the second year still found him at it. I do not

know what would have happened during the third year had I persevered. We surrounded Rauh with a warm and respectful sympathy. Now and then there was a rumor that he had been "converted" to the Durkheimian orthodoxy, but he never really was. Not, at least, during my years at the Sorbonne, and I hardly believe that such a born moralist could have ever substituted sociology for ethics.

Let us leave aside Henri Bergson, who was then teaching at the Collège de France. More about him will be said later. Léon Brunschvicg was to hold the Chair of General Philosophy at the Sorbonne from 1909 to the disasters of the Second World War. In more than one respect his teaching was to have on the minds of students an influence that is still perceptible today. Sartre's existentialist reaction against the idealism and optimism of Brunschvicg is a sure proof of the influence it exercised on the minds of students during the period between the two world wars. Brunschvicg lived up to the noble title of his chair, and he was the only one at the University of Paris to teach a philosophy comparable in its scope to that of Bergson. We should also mention here Félix Alcan, who provided this French philosophical revival with the publishing house it needed, and Élie Halévy, cofounder of the *Revue de métaphysique et de morale* with Xavier Léon—the little man with a big heart, of unlimited generosity in all domains, whose memory is dear to all who have known him. Xavier Léon did not content himself with keeping his journal open and free. He even opened his home to young philosophers; it became for them the center of a philosophical family to which, after so many tragic years, the survivors still feel that they belong.

Politics played no part in all these relationships. Anti-Dreyfusism and Combism were then past their peak, and my generation was fortunate enough to live those years of study with no other care than to bring them to a happy completion. We would make no distinction whatever between those of our masters who were Jews and those who, like Brochard, Delbos, Séailles, Egger, and Lalande, were either pure Greek rationalists, Protestants, or Catholics. Lachelier and Boutroux were still alive, but they were rarely seen; they were heard still less, and they were hardly read at all. Nothing distinguished our masters from one another in the free exercise of reason. It is only from our present distance from these events that what seemed then of no significance now appears to suggest a pattern. Until the time of Bergson and Brunschvicg, France did not have a Spinoza. How many philosophers belonging to the same ethnic group have taught at the University of Paris? I do not mean in France before the Revolution, but simply since the first years of the twentieth century. There must be some reason to account for the fact that these birds, once so rare, arrived in the course of one generation, in a flock and, as it were, at one flight.

One cannot pretend that our masters taught us a uniform doctrine. Since we shall often refer to "Christian philosophy" in this book, it may be wise to stipulate at once that it would be wrong to attribute to those of our masters who were Jews anything like a "Jewish philosophy." To do so would be like painting a blind window on a wall in order to match a real one. I know that there have been Jewish philosophers; my point is that the only metaphysics inspired by the Jewish revelation I happen to know is the work of Christians. To be sure, their Jewish education had an impact on the thinking of the masters whose names I have just recalled, but instead of resorting to philosophy for a better understanding of their religious faith, as Christian philosophers do, the Jews I have known used philosophy to liberate themselves from their religion. Christians philosophize to identify themselves more intimately with their Christianity; our masters philosophized in order to run away from the synagogue. The illustrious example of Spinoza is a typical instance of what I mean. After the *Theologico-Political Treatise,* written as a farewell to the Law, its commands and its rites, came the *Ethica,* whose purpose was to create a mental universe in which reason was liberated from all contact with any religious revelation, Jewish or Christian. It would seem that the philosophical conversion of such children of Israel consists in turning their backs on their religion.

I know of nothing more significant in this respect than two statements of Bergson recently quoted by Claude Tresmontant. One is taken from a letter to Vladimir Jankélévitch: "I think I have told you that I always feel somewhat at home when I read again the *Ethica,* and this regularly surprises me, since most of my own fundamental positions seem to be (and indeed are) in complete opposition to Spinozism." The other is the astonishing profession of faith made to Léon Brunschvicg on the occasion of the two hundred and fiftieth anniversary of the death of the Amsterdam philosopher: "Every philosopher has two philosophies, his own and Spinoza's." The surprise experienced by Bergson is even more revealing than his words. To account for it, Bergson looked toward philosophy and, of course, found no light there, for something else was at stake. Had he only said: "Every Jewish thinker who philosophizes has two philosophies, his own and Spinoza's," the answer to his puzzle would have been plain enough to him.

The doctrines of these university professors were

really quite different from one another. Even the personal philosophy of Lévy-Bruhl did not coincide exactly with that of Durkheim, while Frédéric Rauh was going his own way, perhaps parallel to theirs, but still different from them. The only element common to their doctrines is a negative one, but nonetheless real and very active in its own order. One might describe it as a radical defiance of all that which is social conceived as a constraint from which to be liberated. Spinoza and Brunschvicg achieved this liberation through metaphysics, Durkheim and Lévy-Bruhl through science and sociology, Bergson through intuition, by breaking through at the top: his "open" religion carried him beyond the confining limits of a religion that was "closed." Against the Law, Judaism can always appeal to the Prophets. But among all these doctrines the one that bears most visibly the marks of its religious origins may very well be that of Léon Brunschvicg. Not unlike Spinoza, whom he held in such affection and esteem, Brunschvicg in his philosophy constantly protested against Judaism, which he was fond of denouncing even under its Christian form. His philosophy was a substanceless Spinozism, for it was a religion of the refusal of the object. The philosophy of Brunschvicg progressively assumed the colors of a religion because, far from being itself an object, the knowing spirit fulfilled a function similar to that of the *élan vital* in the philosophy of Bergson. It was the creative force at work in science, which ceaselessly went on leaving behind itself all the concepts, dogmas, and institutions that it created and surpassed.

As the years went by, Léon Brunschvicg spoke more and more the language of a theologian, even of a religious reformer. He would distinguish between a true conversion, which was a conversion to his own philosophy of the spirit, and a false conversion, which was that of the believer's conversion to God. Despite my affection for him, I must confess that at times I felt annoyed to hear myself taxed with atheism *because* I believed in the existence of God. And indeed, in his own view of the problem, to conceive God as a person was the same as to conceive Him as a thing, which amounted to negating Him. Brunschvicg progressively locked himself up within the walls of a city of the spirit, narrow as all human spirits are, but which looked immense to him because he never tired of circling it. To him the task of philosophy was precisely to discern the spirit in its purity, to serve it, and to give to the world souls dedicated to truth and justice. As a professor, he made it a duty to multiply such souls. He had no other aim in his conversation, which was but a more familiar form of his teaching, slow, flowing but measured, (as often as not accompanying walks that could be long), or unceremoniously cutting with replies— "No, it is not like that"—expressed in a manner that was always peremptory but never harsh. With Brunschvicg I often felt as though I was on the fringe of a selected group of pure spirits that I never managed to join. Indeed Brunschvicg would concede to me the Gospel of Saint John, but not that of Saint Matthew: the Word, not Jesus Christ. What he objected to in Christianity was what it had retained of Judaism.

And yet Brunschvicg himself, with the simplicity that never failed him, sometimes would tell a friend about the decisive moment in his life when he had liberated himself from Judaism. It was a time of fasting. To make sure that he was not simply yielding to the temptation of a very natural desire for food, but asserting his independence from the Law, the young philosopher ate one bean. He would emphasize the word *one,* for in his mind the insignificance of the *corpus delicti* guaranteed the purity of his intention. I tried in vain to make him understand that in binding him so closely to the letter of the Law, Leviticus had scored once more. What is a cult in spirit and truth to which a man can dedicate himself by eating one bean, but one only?

One should not pretend then that these masters were teaching a Jewish philosophy in the sense that has been defined above. Far from considering himself bound to the religion of Israel, each one of them believed he was thinking as a pure philosopher, free from all opinions not exclusively rational. To this extent a sort of pre-established harmony marked them out as the philosophers of a godless State. Protecting with care their philosophical thinking from all religious influence, they naturally expected others to do the same. Much later, when I had become a professor at the Sorbonne, one of them requested my presence for an important message. He had been told that I took advantage of my teaching of the history of medieval philosophies to carry on a religious propaganda. I owed him so much that he had every right to ask me such a question; but I must say that the question left me flabbergasted. He did not want me to justify myself; a simple denial on my part would have been enough for him. But I have always thought that in order to teach any doctrine, a historian should present it in the fullness of its intelligibility, and how can he show that a philosophy is intelligible without somehow justifying it? I have no objection to criticizing doctrines, but legitimate as it is, criticism is not history, it is philosophy. Not knowing what to answer, I immediately offered to exchange at the first occasion my Chair of the History of Medieval Philosophy for a Chair of the History of Modern Philosophy. After all, I was not without title to it. The change would at least have given me the pleasure of explaining Descartes, Comte, or Hegel without being suspected of conducting secret propaganda in their favor. The offer was neither accepted nor ever renewed and the matter was dropped.

I have reported this anecdote first because it constitutes the complete account of the persecutions I suffered in the University of Paris for having publicly expounded the doctrine of Saint Thomas Aquinas as I understood it. I served the University to the best of my ability, in the way she wanted to be served. And I am infinitely grateful to her for having accepted me such as I was. Had God granted me the grace to teach Saint Thomas Aquinas in the Order of Saint Dominic, I might have fared worse.

This incident illustrates the situation of my masters at the Sorbonne between 1904 and 1907. One day Léon Brunschvicg took me aside and said: "I want to show you something that will give you pleasure." It was a letter in which Jules Lachelier reminded his correspondent that, for him, there were religious dogmas and that they played a part in his philosophy. Thus did I learn, long after my student years, that Lachelier was a Catholic. I had never known it until then. Was Victor Delbos a Catholic? It was rumored, but nothing in his teaching or in his writings would permit anyone to affirm it. The Christian faith was as absent from their public thinking as the Old Testament and the synagogue were from the lectures or the writings of Émile Durkheim. This teaching wished to be religiously "neutral," as they say, and it was to the fullest possible extent; with this disturbing consequence, however, that our masters agreed chiefly on negations, abstentions, or tacit reservations, so that few among them felt free to teach those truths that were to them highest and dearest.

The result was a very special situation for philosophy itself. To insure all the more scrupulously its religious "neutrality," our masters restricted philosophy to those disciplines which, tending to establish themselves into so many separate sciences, broke away more and more completely from all metaphysics and even more from all religion. Psychology became both physiology and psychiatry, logic was a methodology, ethics made way for the *science des moeurs;* sociology tried to do away with even the master problems of metaphysics by interpreting them as the collective representations they were supposed to be. No chair of metaphysics, of course; still, since it is awkward to maintain in a university a department of philosophy without having something to put under this word, an answer to the problem was found in the decision to teach, by way of philosophy, that there is no such thing as philosophy. To teach philosophy as though metaphysics does not exist is itself a philosophical program. Thus the *Critique of Pure Reason* became the charter of a philosophical training of which it fully justified the negativist direction. Year after year Victor Delbos commented on the text for students, while Lucien Lévy-Bruhl was responsible for the *Critique of Practical Reason.* They used to the same purpose the so-called absolute positivism, which did not even go to the trouble of philosophizing in order to prove that one should not philosophize. Aristotle himself would have been at a loss to answer it. Born of the disintegration of Comtism, "absolute positivism" was more a state of mind than a doctrine. It simply took it for granted that, apart from the positive sciences, there was no knowledge worthy of the name. This did not need to be proved: it was evident. Under the name of philosophy such a pure scientism taught the more general conclusions reached in the various sciences, as if the interpretation of science could be the work of anyone but scientists themselves. In the end both criticism and scientific positivism agreed on this point, of paramount importance in their eyes, that the problems of the world, of the soul, and of God were out of date. Provided you granted them this triple negation, they were satisfied.

Today it is hard to recapture this state of mind. I still remember the day—it was, I believe, in the Turgot auditorium—when, under the strain of his burning sincerity, Frédéric Rauh blurted out the confession that "there are times when one feels almost ashamed to call oneself a philosopher." This upset me greatly. What was I doing there, I who had no other reason to be there than the love of philosophy? Rauh's words reminded me of the advice I had received from another one of my masters at the beginning of my philosophical studies. "So you are interested in religion and art? Very well, but this can wait. For the time being, study the sciences." "Which sciences?" "Any sciences. Provided they be sciences, they will teach you what it is to *know.*"

There was something sound in that advice, but when science is applied to art and religion, the result is neither art nor religion; it is science. There appeared to be no other choice then than either to get a smattering of the sciences without mastering any one, which was unprofitable, or else to dedicate a whole life to the study of one science, a thing excellent in itself but not easily reconciled with any rewarding reflection on the problems of art or religion. We did not fail to realize the difficulty. A way of escape had to be found. It lay in the history of philosophy. Why not learn from Plato, or Descartes, or any other great "thinker of the past" the way to ask and to answer metaphysical questions?

And yet there was an argument against doing so; it was precisely that ever since the reformation achieved by Kant and Comte, all preceding philosophies had been rendered obsolete. The historian of philosophy thus found himself acting as the caretaker of the cemetery of dead metaphysics. My friend Professor Bush of Columbia University had a charming phrase to describe this avocation: mental archaeology. In more recent years, I have often met similar expressions from the pens of philosophers and theologians giving vent, less elegantly but no less firmly, to their hostility toward historical research. This opposition would be harmless if it did not so often indicate on the part of such persons the intention to discuss history without knowing it. In 1905 the situation was different, since people really did want to study the history of philosophy. However, they did so only inasmuch as it dealt with doctrines that still had something useful to say because, from the first moment of their conception, what they taught was *already* true.

This preoccupation affected history in a twofold way. First, in the choice of the philosophies studied. I do not recall having attended a lecture course on Aristotle; but Plato, the father of idealism, was regularly taught. Descartes announced positivism and Hume criticism; both were therefore important philosophers. The same preoccupation affected even the interpretation of the doctrines that for different reasons had been retained. The history of philosophy, such as it was then taught, did not especially stress what had interested the philosophers themselves, but rather what was considered important in its own right in philosophy. One obtained thus a Descartes occupied with a method that was declared excellent simply because it was mathematical, even though the metaphysics and physics that derived from it were, to say the least, doubtful or even false. What they were looking for in Descartes toward 1900 was the forerunner of scientism. No one asked what Descartes himself would have said had he been told: "Your method is indeed excellent, but the conclusions you derive from it are worthless." Students were also introduced to a Malebranche without theology, to a logicized Leibniz who had lost his interest in the religious organization of the earth. When, in a memorable book, Jean Baruzi made clear that this problem lay at the heart of Leibniz' thought, no one paid any attention to it. And, indeed, this was a religious problem and had nothing to do with philosophy. But perhaps the most remarkable manifestation of this state of mind was the treatment accorded the philosophy of Auguste Comte. He too, and perhaps he especially, had dedicated his life to the religious organization of humanity. In his own words, he had wanted to begin as Aristotle in order to become Saint Paul. This gigantic program came to very little in the hands of his historians. It became a positive philosophy without a positive politics and positive religion, in short the positivism of Littré rather than that of Comte, and moreover a positivism that was mutilated and reduced to the introductory lectures on the classification of sciences or on the method and object of sociology. Comte was thus turned into the prophet of Durkheim, which he could not be without ceasing to be Comte. At any rate, it was impossible to expect either a philosophy of religion or a metaphysics from a history that was no more than the

agony of religion and metaphysics. We had arrived at
the wrong time. We wanted to enter the temple at the
very moment the priests were closing the doors.

This negative appraisal of the situation would give a
false idea of the place given to philosophy at the Sorbonne in the first years of the century, if we did not
balance it by stressing the extraordinary liberalism that
inspired such teaching. Negative it certainly was, but
it was in no way destructive. Charles Péguy, a shrewd
contemporary observer, has remarked that at a time
when each department of the Faculty of Letters in the
University of Paris had its great authority—Brunot for
grammar, Lanson for French literature, Lavisse for
history, Andler for Germanic studies—the department
of philosophy had none. "The queen of all the disciplines," said Péguy, "has no presiding genius in the
Sorbonne. It is a remarkable fact that philosophy is
not represented in the assembly of the gods, that it has
no great authority in the Sorbonne."

This was true. When I recall those faraway years, I
realize that our masters constituted a republic and
thereby made it possible for us to enjoy the benefit of
a republican regime, a form of government whose
merits are open to discussion at the level of politics, but
which certainly is the best one, or rather the only possible one, on the dual level of science and philosophy.
Our masters may well have told us *how*, in their opinion, we should think, but not one of them ever pre-
sumed to tell us *what* we should think. No authoritarian
regime, no established church, would have so scrupulously respected our intellectual freedom. In times like
ours, which are a witness to the triumph of dirigistic
regimes, one feels reluctant to underrate a state of
affairs that is so hard to resurrect once it has ceased to
exist. "It is evident," said Péguy, "that M. Durkheim

is not at all a presiding genius *of* philosophy, but *against* philosophy." Let us rather say Durkheim was such a genius *for* sociology such as he himself understood it and whose triumph he naturally awaited. He was so sure of this triumph that he felt no need to be *against* anything, not even metaphysics. Péguy had an epic mind. Personally I was never aware of that "fear of all that which pertains to thinking" with which Péguy taxed the Sorbonne of 1913. On the contrary, and this is not a little thing, we were left the task of seeking for ourselves our intellectual bread and of reconquering by ourselves what we should have received as our just inheritance. Would it be so dear to us today if we had not had to work so hard for it? A pointless question indeed, since in history we cannot really know what might have happened. Of what did actually happen, one thing at least is certain: that the much abused Sorbonne instilled in us a love for work well done, as well as an absolute respect for truth. There was no one to teach us the truth, but no one forbade us to express it. In sum, and this is no light praise, our youth had no other burden to carry than that of our freedom.

CONFUSION IN THE CITY

During my three years of study at the Sorbonne I had not lost contact with my former masters and friends at Notre-Dame-des-Champs. If I were writing my memoirs, I should want to name more than one. However, there is one person whose presence in this book is necessary because of the decisive part he played in the history of my own thinking.

From the faraway past, slightly before the First World War, which Péguy kept prophesying but which most intellectuals refused to believe possible, there emerges the face of a young priest. He was of medium height and spare figure, with a high forehead, intense eyes, a face that narrowed abruptly, and a thin mouth from which came an unforgettably warm voice. Every inch a priest. He greeted you as a brother and, though young, he was already endowed with a spiritual maturity that qualified him to be our guide.

Director and professor of philosophy at the Great Seminary of Issy, the Abbé Lucien Paulet was soon to be invited to look for other duties. I knew that this was bound to happen on the day he told me, still shaking with indignation, that at dinner one of the "Messieurs de Saint-Sulpice" had spoken of Bergson in a slighting way. "I told him quite clearly what I thought!" my friend said. It was easy to foresee what would happen. A born philosopher, unable to compromise, he had but one course and that was to resign—which he did. This noble man, whose heart burned with the love of Christ, took up parish work without feeling in any way diminished. When the war broke out in 1914, the Abbé Paulet volunteered as a chaplain for shock troops. Knowing full well that during attacks death was a permanent threat, but acting on the principle that a chaplain should be present wherever soldiers die, he always went with his men under fire with no other weapon than his crucifix and no other desire than to give absolution. A bullet in the head put a premature end to his life, so filled with sacrifices accepted in joyful love. "He has shed His blood for us," this priest of Christ would say, "let us shed ours." Those who have loved him still love him. They pray to him in the secret depth of their hearts. It has never even occurred to them that they should pray for him.

As one can easily believe, the difficulties of the Abbé Paulet were not without a cause. If one were to look for an epitaph to be inscribed on his tomb, two words would suffice: Lucien Paulet (1876–1915), Priest, Bergsonian. He was both with undivided heart. The love of Christ and of the Cross, the love of truth, the veneration for our common master, all blended into one single feeling whose ultimate object was God. Deeply versed in the writings of Bergson, he spontaneously prolonged their meaning, beyond their immediate conclusions, toward the mysteries of a religion foreign to the mind of the philosopher himself, but of which his teaching seemed to have an obscure presentiment.

How many hours we spent in passionate conversation on the last lecture of Bergson or on the last book we had just read! One would not go and see Bergson. It was not done. How could we monopolize even an hour in a life whose every minute was precious to all? But we felt for him a very personal devotion, using the word in the beautiful sense our ancestors gave to it, of loving gratitude for all his gifts.

Among the topics of our conversations, there was one that recurred with particular frequency. Usually it was introduced by my friend. Although I never heard him speak of Bergson as of a Christian, and he was clearly conscious of the distance there still was between *Creative Evolution* and Holy Scripture, the Abbé Paulet was nonetheless impressed with the analogy, imperfect but unmistakable, between the Bergsonian view of the world and Christian creationism. With more generosity than prudence, he undertook to teach his seminarians a Bergsonizing scholasticism, which to him was the true philosophy. This was a risky undertaking and certainly a premature one at a time when, not having written *The Two Sources of Morality and Religion,* Bergson himself had still to say his last word on the subject. In any case, my friend was not indiscreet enough to put words in Bergson's mouth and make him speak as a Christian. He was speaking in his own name and, as I listened to him, I admired the inspired warmth of his interpretation. The doctrine of Bergson seemed to grow in depth and boldness as though quickened from within by new blood. Looking at these events from a distance, it seems evident to me today that this young master could not be allowed to improvise a new scholasticism at the price of risk to himself as well as to his students. It is not permissible to err in teaching young clerics. Canon Law imposes on them the study of a philosophy so closely connected with their theology that the one can scarcely be rejected without imperiling the other. The ghost of this scholastic philosophy, which for my friend was to be exorcised from the classrooms of seminaries, came up again and again in our conversations, and it was always he who brought it back. It was his *delenda Carthago.* Personally I was in complete ignorance of it. My teachers at Notre-Dame-des-Champs had taught me my religion very well, but they had not confused it with scholasticism. As for the Sorbonne, it had taught me only two things in this matter, namely, that scholasticism was a philosophy that need not be known since Descartes had overthrown it, and that moreover one had its exact measure when he knew that it was a misinterpretation of Aristotelianism. I have always wondered whether it was a good thing or a misfortune that I was never taught scholastic philosophy. The answer depends on the kind of scholasticism I would have been taught. This, at least, seems certain: that had I been exposed in my youth to the kind of scholastic philosophy represented by the textbooks then in use in the schools, such teaching would have been for me a genuine catastrophe. Recalling the experience of several I have known, I should be tempted to say it would have been an irreparable misfortune.

Let us pause a moment to consider what scholasticism is, not indeed in itself and at the peak of its perfection, but such as it presented itself to my mind in the barren form in which it was taught at the Grand Séminaire of Paris. To hear it so much attacked made me curious to know the monster. I secured a copy of the manual then in use at Issy. The two small volumes are still in my possession. They are the *Elementa Philosophiae Scholasticae* by Sébastien Reinstadler, published in 1904 by Herder in Freiburg (Breisgau) as well as in several other places, including St. Louis in the United States. I do not distinctly remember the impressions these volumes made on me at the time, except I know that they revealed to me a completely foreign country.

As a student I was familiar with other philosophical methods, but I could not open these volumes without being greatly surprised. It was not so much the doctrine that disturbed me, since I myself had nothing precise enough in mind to be upset by it. Nor were the conclusions of Reinstadler any different from mine. A young Catholic spontaneously finds himself in a much more complete agreement with any form of scholasticism than he will ever be with Hume, Kant, or Comte. What really disturbed me was that these volumes, which claimed to give an account of *philosophy*—a point not to be forgotten—drew their inspiration from a source entirely foreign to those of other philosophies. True, the other philosophies contradicted one another often enough, but they were not based upon any a priori refusal to communicate among themselves. They rather believed in dialogue. On the contrary, in the scholastic philosophy of the schools, every main part of Reinstadler's manual concluded with a series of ringing refutations. It was a case of scholasticism against all comers.

To grasp the exact nature of the doctrine was nevertheless difficult. To repeat, the general conclusions were perfectly clear but they did not teach us anything we did not already know. There is only one God, infinite, all powerful, an immovable yet creative spiritual substance, and so on; but we had already learned all this from our catechism even before our first communion. On the other hand, the author claimed to be following Aristotle, who had held none of these conclusions. Reinstadler could have limited himself to teaching the authentic conclusions of Aristotle, but then there would not have been any infinite and unique God, Creator of heaven and earth, exercising His care over the smallest of His creatures, nor would there have been for man a personal immortality of the soul. To avoid these awkward results, Reinstadler preferred to teach a body of Aristotelian tenets topped off by the master conclusions of Christian philosophy. Divided according to the tradition of Wolff rather than that of Aristotle and Saint Thomas, this manual refused to take the other philosophies into consideration. Not that Reinstadler refused to speak about them, nor was he incapable of understanding them. Far from it. His exposition of Kant was as good as could be reasonably expected from that type of book. But he made absolutely no effort to understand the motives behind these philosophies. Reinstadler never judged their answers in the light of the problems the philosophers had attempted to solve. For him the main point was to demonstrate that the philosophy of Kant was false.

Outside the restricted society of scholastics, very few practice this kind of philosophizing. An excerpt from Reinstadler may help to show more clearly the revulsion experienced by a student of the Sorbonne to the high-handed method of a judge who, not content to find other philosophies guilty, went on to insult them. The precise case at stake is that of Kant. "All critique resulting in the negation of truths universally accepted because their evidence is obvious to the mind, or in the affirmation of what everyone naturally denies and rejects as false in the conduct of life, is itself not only false but utterly insane (*dementissima*). Now such is the Kantian *Critique of Pure Reason*, for all its conclusions are contrary to common sense, to the natural judgment of the mind, and to all that men do and say. Hence the criticism of Kant should be rejected as something insane (*ergo criticismus kantianus ut insania reiciendus est*)."

This is only one instance. In the course of its long history, for the most part devoted to controversy, modern scholasticism has not only picked up the debris of the many doctrines that it passed through, it also contracted some of their bad habits. Among others, let us mention the bad manners introduced into controversy by the worst enemies of scholasticism, the humanists of the sixteenth century. Any conclusion that Sanseverino rejects is absurd: *Absurdus est modus quo Kantius criticam suam confirmare studet . . . ; absurdam doctrinam asserit Fichtaeus . . . ; haec superiorum Germaniae philosophorum systemata omnino absurda esse ab iis quae alibi demonstravimus satis patet,* and so on. He is always doing it. Only the scholastic philosophers writing in Latin still think that insult is a step in an argument. They themselves are not really angry and they do not mean any mischief. These insults are to them literary ornaments, the mere suggestion of a dance step at the torture pole. The poor man is wrong, hence he is out of his wits.

These philosophical manners were astonishing to me. I was even scandalized by them at the time, and all the more so as their meaning and point escaped me. Today no one reads a treatise in scholastic philosophy unless he is professionally bound to do so. This is a mistake, since some of them are very interesting; but the knowledge of this very fact surrounds with a kind of insularity those authors for whom scholastic philosophy is the only true one. Their readers, they know, will share their ideas, whereas those whom they treat so cavalierly will not read them. Why be concerned? This is a conversation between friends and behind closed doors. Admission is not forbidden, but the well-known fact is that nobody wants to come in.

The true reason for their attitude lies elsewhere and concerns the very nature of their philosophy. The authors of these treatises claim to be philosophers, and so they are, but all of them are likewise theologians. They are even primarily theologians, because a theologian is always first and before anything else a theologian. All the authors who write such philosophical treatises have completed their philosophical formation by a theological training. But their philosophical education itself was already directed toward theology and already informed by it; so much so that, on coming back to philosophy, they cannot again resume a purely philosophical out-

look. Now a theologian passes judgment and he condemns; this is one of his functions, and Saint Thomas
did not fail to do so: *Ac per hoc excluditur error di-
centium.* He condemns error in theology, but he also
does it in philosophy every time that directly or indi-
rectly its consequences place the teaching of faith in
jeopardy. Nothing is more legitimate, except that the
Elementa Philosophiae Scholasticae and the like claim
to be treatises in philosophy, not theology. Quite apart
from the question of courtesy, the philosopher does
not condemn by way of authority; he refutes by rational
argument. This is much less easy. To reduce the doctrine of Kant to one "proposition" and to deduce its condemnation by pure syllogistic reasoning, this is the true
method of theology. It is appropriate in theology, but
in philosophy the difficulty always lies with the major
premise. *If* the philosophy of Kant contradicts all the
principles of speculative and practical reason, then it is
a false philosophy indeed. But one scarcely needs to be
a Kantian in order to see that this proposition itself
would be difficult to prove. I am not a Kantian, and I
have never been tempted to become one; moreover,
I fully recognize the right and the duty of a theologian
to condemn Kantism as incompatible with the teaching
of the Church. But then one should not claim to be
making a purely philosophical judgment. For if Kantism
is an insanity, it is one that has affected many philosophers, and when one feels surrounded by madmen, it is
prudent to seek professional advice.

We deeply felt the danger in those faraway days, but
we did not know its cause. The Abbé Lucien Paulet
found it trying to be among colleagues who made such
short theological work of philosophical difficulties. Their
attitude was a satisfying one to them since to condemn
philosophical propositions as contrary to faith is evi-

dently for theologians the surest and most efficient way of getting rid of them. To repeat, in theology the method is perfectly legitimate. All the doctrinal condemnations pronounced by the Church ultimately rest on her religious authority and therefore are not tied to any philosophical justification. All I wish to say is that this method has no place in philosophy as such, all the more so if the philosophy in question is expressly defined and established in itself *prior to* theology and, to that extent, *outside* theology. Good for internal consumptions, this way of settling philosophical disputes is habit-forming and it excludes from the community of philosophers those who extend it to metaphysics. My friend the abbé had met too many philosophers not to know that he had to choose between yielding to that habit and sharing their society. Therefore, when his colleagues and superiors, who themselves had their own reason, made it a matter of conscience for him to philosophize as they did, he realized that he was not in the right place, and it was then he decided to give up teaching philosophy.

They are all dead: our master Bergson, French philosopher; Lucien Paulet himself, priest and Frenchman, killed in action; Charles Péguy, *couché dessus le sol à la face de Dieu,* the one among us all who loved and understood Bergsonism best and in its most intimate implications; Pierre Rousselot, S.J., the herald of that revival of the authentic Thomism of Saint Thomas Aquinas that was to liberate us from so many uncertainties, also killed in action, buried in the mud of the Eparges, as a true Jesuit who kept nothing to himself, not even his own body. Gone. Vanished. Nothing. The purity of their sacrifice does not console us for such losses. Nothing will give us back the spiritual riches that we would have received from them had they lived. Such elders would have known how to graft a Bergsonian branch on the ancient but still vigorous trunk of scholasticism. The life of my friend was cut short, but he was robbed even more of a genuine scholasticism.

This needs to be said. Here precisely lay the root of the evil in those confused years of the modernist crisis when nothing could be put back in its place because the place had ceased to exist. No doubt we were wrong in mistaking for true scholasticism what was only a decadent and degenerate model. But how could those who were in error have been rescued from it when their critics, who were right, did not know exactly why they were right? I have often wondered about what would have happened if a Lucien Paulet had been enlightened on the true meaning of Thomism, that is to say, if he had known the metaphysics of being as taught by Thomas Aquinas himself, which so often differs from what his disciples attribute to him. I have no doubt that today my friend would be an ardent Thomist. He would have found in Thomas much more than the best that Bergson was ever able to offer us. But my friend died without ever suspecting what Thomistic metaphysics really is. I myself had no idea of it, and even now I search my memory in vain to find in it, among the philosophers I then knew the name of someone who could have told me what it was. For, as much as I can today understand the modernist disorder in philosophy, it was primarily that failure. There would not have been so many of us in error if the elders who should have been our guides had been more completely right.

I have no intention of shifting responsibility. Modernism was a bundle of errors and those who held them were responsible for them. But a responsibility of a different sort weighed on those who, through their own fault, allowed truth to be so often ignored or misunderstood in the first place. They themselves had misrepresented it to such a degree that it could no longer be recognized as such.

On the street car from Saint-Mandé to Paris, a priest with stooping shoulders and a worried expression on his face was taking to task a young philosopher friend whom he had just met by chance. They were at the end of the line, the car was almost empty and the few passengers waiting for it to leave the station were amused to see this man filled with a strange excitement and endlessly repeating: "It's a square circle! It's a square circle!" This priest of the Oratory of Jesus was thus upbraiding the Thomists for teaching a notion that was a veritable monstrosity, namely, the notion of *an-Aristotelian-nature-in-a-state-of-grace.* He would have been right if nature as Saint Thomas conceived it had been an Aristotelian nature, which it is not. The indignation of Father Lucien Laberthonnière had no object, but he could not guess it. He had been taught that the philosophy of Saint Thomas and that of Aristotle were one and the same. He therefore believed it, but he would not have been any more satisfied had the situation been different. Were Thomism a philosophy in any proper sense, it would have displeased him. It was the very same Father Laberthonnière who thought that even Édouard Le Roy and Maurice Blondel placed too much confidence in philosophy. He himself seemed to have taken literally the famous words of Saint Augustine: true religion is true philosophy and, in its turn, true philosophy is true religion.

These thoughts would sometimes cross my mind as I listened to Father Laberthonnière, but apart from the fact that it has always been difficult to reduce his thought to a few clear-cut formulas, I still hesitate to believe that he really wanted to do away with philosophy as distinct from religion. At any rate, I found it difficult to share his violent opposition to Thomas Aquinas. To begin with, I felt an aversion toward being in opposition to the authority of the Church. It was unlikely that the Church erred to that extent in the choice of a Common Doctor and of a Patron of all the Catholic Schools. Three propositions claimed my attention at the same time: the Church of Rome is the true Church; Thomas Aquinas, as Father Laberthonnière sometimes said, has done more harm to the Church than Luther; in philosophy as in theology the norm of the teaching of the Church is the doctrine of Thomas Aquinas. One or another of these propositions could be true, they could not all be true together.

I had another source of anxiety. This Thomas Aquinas, the scapegoat of scholasticism, was much talked about and many views were expressed in his name, but his words were not often quoted and, when they were, the notions attributed to him sounded strange. This was disturbing to us, but not to his critics. If a quotation expressed some fantastic idea or other, then it certainly was authentically Thomistic. One of the objections then leveled at Saint Thomas was that he turned God into a thing. It therefore looked quite natural when in 1907 Édouard Le Roy declared in *Dogme et Critique* that according to the Common Doctor of the Church, God was not only someone unknown (*ignotus*) but something unknown (*ignotum*). What beginner in Latin could write such nonsense: *Deus est ignotum?* In fact, Thomas Aquinas never wrote it. Thus Thomas' doctrine of the divine unknowability, which forbids us not only that we should imagine God as a thing, but that we should imagine Him at all, was grossly disfigured and even turned against the intention of its author. But as I said, the more unlikely the formula, the more believable it was. Father Laberthonnière would not miss such an opportunity. Saint Thomas, he observed with relish, was not satisfied to say *Deus est ignotus:* God is not known; he said: God is an-I-know-not-what: *Deus est ignotum.* They did not bother to do justice to this hateful theologian. Nothing was beyond him.

The consequences of such a state of mind were serious. Father Laberthonnière's own position on all problems had become colored by his fierce hatred of Aristotelian scholasticism. Fully alive to the differences that distinguish the philosophy of Aristotle from Christian teaching, and rightly indignant that they were often confused, he himself was not satisfied to distinguish them—he wanted to set them in opposition. He has developed this idea in what remains to my mind the best of his books, *Christian Realism and Greek Idealism,* published in 1904. Along with excellent things, the reader will find in it a Chapter IV entitled "Opposition Between Christianity and Greek Philosophy," followed by Chapter V in which is explained the ground of the conflict between Greek reason and Christian faith: "It is in themselves and by themselves that they are opposed, so much so that if one is true the other is an illusion." Such views were hard to swallow. While it was impossible for me to grant that the philosophy of Aristotle was *already* a Christian philosophy of a sort, I found it no less surprising to hear that the Philosopher, who could know nothing of Christianity, taught a doctrine *already* in opposition with the Christian revelation. Aristotelianism can mean to Christianity only what it means in the mind of a Christian theologian. One could well wonder, therefore, whether the conflict denounced by Father Laberthonnière had a reality outside his own mind. Seen today from a distance, what happened then was simple enough: Father Laberthonnière detested Saint Thomas Aquinas because of Aristotle, but he detested Aristotle even more because of Saint Thomas Aquinas. The situation was more confused in those days. As for me, what I saw before anything else was a priest whose soul was torn apart by this opposition to the Church in which his zeal for the same Church had placed him, and who was in agony.

Perplexities of this nature could not wipe out the impression left on young minds by such a strong conviction in a priest of such purity of life and exemplary piety who was fighting in defense of religion. It is no wonder that when several of his books were placed on the Index, and this step was followed by the cruel interdiction to teach and to publish, his friends were left in confusion. Nothing could make him change his way of thinking. On the contrary, he could only yield more and more to the strange obsession that was the constant companion of his solitude. In this solitude, I never heard him utter a single word of defiance or a single complaint. His submission to the Church was exemplary. Far from exciting to rebellion those of his friends who were indignant at the severity of the sentence, he never ceased urging them to be patient and to respect discipline. Somewhat later events were going to increase the disorder, which spread from theology to politics and from speculation to action.

I had just begun my teaching career when Pope Pius X condemned the Sillon. This was in 1910 and I felt deeply affected by it. I should like to try to explain why, but I am not sure that I shall succeed.

I had never seen Marc Sangnier, I had never attended any meeting of the Sillon, and to this day I have never read a single article from his pen. I did not belong to the Sillon, nor for that matter to any political party, but there were many of us who felt very close to Marc Sangnier and at one with him in his struggle. The only thing we knew, and it was enough for us, was that, in opposition to those who considered the Church as inseparably linked to an old monarchical regime, Sangnier wanted to establish in France a Catholicism that was socially minded and loyal to the Republic. Leo XIII wanted at least political freedom for Catholics. Quite apart from all doctrine, our hearts leaned toward Marc Sangnier. Most of us were Christians and republicans belonging to the middle class. All we knew was that a Christian devoted to the Republic was somewhere fighting for us. The condemnation of his movement was for many of us a thunderbolt. If he did not want to be a royalist, what other party could a French Catholic still join? If there was one, where was it?

Today it is easy to see that the condemnation should not have been interpreted in this way. But I am not writing an apologia, I am trying to relate facts such as they appeared to us at the time, and the fact is that this is how the condemnation was understood. Besides, it was easy to foresee that it would be understood that way. To be fair to those who misinterpreted the event, one must keep in mind the complexity of the situation.

When the sentence was passed, the campaign against the Sillon had been going on for a long time and, following an established tradition, it had started in France. When a Frenchman complains in Rome that his country bears the brunt of ecclesiastical censure, the answer is always the same: Why do your countrymen spend so much time in denouncing one another? The race of informers and of heresy hunters is not dead today, but then the modernist crisis was its golden age. When a Catholic does not agree with another Catholic on any problem, the easiest way to outdo him is to get his position condemned as suspect and, if possible, as erroneous. This does not always work, but when it does, it is most effective. We have often seen it put in practice and witnessed its efficacy.

There was absolutely nothing in common between the philosophy of Father Laberthonnière and the social or political positions of the Sillon. Nevertheless, their adversaries were the same and they had in common two characteristics: most of them claimed to be "Thomists" and, so far as I remember, all of them sided with Charles Maurras. At first glance, this unexpected alliance does not seem to make any sense. The head of Action Française was a professed atheist. Atheists are not rare. Nor was there anything rare in the fact that a political party aimed to use the Church to its own ends, and this is exactly what the Action Française was trying to do. Ever since Auguste Comte's *Appel aux conservateurs* it was well-known that an atheistic positivism could look for political allies among Catholics. Comte had gone one better: he had offered an alliance to the General of the Jesuits. Only in 1856 the Jesuits had not answered the call, whereas between 1906 and 1910 Charles Maurras succeeded in recruiting troops from the ranks of the Jesuits, the Dominicans, and other religious orders.

Posterity will have more leisure than we have, and the future will see things from a distance that is lacking to us. Those who are curious about doctrinal teratology will enjoy unraveling the intricacies of such an alliance. On the political level no explanation is needed. The French people are born fanatics; rightists or leftists, they are always willing to persecute one another in the name of some sacred principle. This time, however, Catholics were the last to have been persecuted. It must be granted that the hideous politics of Combism was not calculated to win religious orders to the Republic, but this is beside the point. The really interesting question was to know why a Master in Theology belonging to

the Order of Saint Dominic, as well as a highly qualified interpreter of Thomism who enjoyed in the Church
an unchallenged doctrinal authority, should then have
felt duty bound to teach that Charles Maurras and Saint
Thomas Aquinas agreed on the notion of "the best political regime."

It is enough to open the *Summa Theologiae* at the
right place to know that this is not true. Yet this theologian was very far from being alone in his error. Laymen of great intelligence and talent did not hesitate
to side quite openly with the "party of order." The heart
of the problem would be to know how, by what secret
channels, Thomism could seem to them to offer a theological justification of the political theory of Charles
Maurras. What the royalists hoped to gain from such
an alliance is obvious. Saint Thomas is the Common
Doctor of the Church. To establish that his political
doctrine was the same as that of Charles Maurras
amounted to proving that the political doctrine of
Charles Maurras was that of the Church. With this
proved, all French Catholics without exception would
have been held in conscience to accept the monarchist
politics of the Action Française. What a haul! Let us re-
sist the temptation to ask what peculiar brand of "Thomism" this must have been to feel akin to the positivism
of Maurras which, like that of Comte, was deeply interested in Rome but not in Jerusalem.

We who were living those events had neither the
leisure nor the means to submit them to such an analysis, but some incidents were in themselves too striking
to pass unnoticed. Let us also acknowledge that both
sides were looking for trouble. The *Annales de philosophie chrétienne* were not wanting in aggressiveness, but
what brought about a premature ending is clear enough.
When Father Laberthonnière took Father Pedro Des-

coqs, S.J., to task on the issue of the Action Française, I knew at once that he was doomed. It may well be that the two facts were not related. As I have already said, I am not pretending to write the history of what did happen, but rather of what we then thought was happening. This is not necessarily the same thing. I am now absolutely sure of this and I know I was not the only one to foresee it. In 1911 Father Laberthonnière published a short pamphlet of forty-two pages entitled *Autour de l'Action Française.* His friends have always been convinced that his adversaries have never forgiven him this action.

Every doctrinal condemnation by the Church is always a religious act. In spite of appearances to the contrary, politics has nothing to do with it; the same is not necessarily true of the motives of those who instigate such condemnations. Looking at the events from the outside, we could not help being impressed by this confluence of heterogeneous interests. How were we to choose? The priests whom we knew personally, because they were part of the world of the philosophers, and whose religious zeal we admired, were sooner or later repudiated by the Church, but those who triumphed over them in the name of orthodoxy either were atheists or appealed to a scholastic philosophy whose language was not that of our day. We were victims of a disorder whose cause we did not know. It is curious that our master Victor Delbos, then a professor at the Sorbonne, expressed at the end of his life his surprise that it took him so many years, even though he was a Catholic, to rediscover the meaning of the ancient notion of wisdom. The generation before ours seems to have experienced some sort of frustration, the feeling of a loss and the desire to restore what was lost. The acute crisis through which our generation passed was not entirely sterile.

It obliged us to enter upon a long inquiry into the causes of misunderstandings that brought into conflict brothers otherwise united in the same faith. A road thirty years long was then opening before us. Had we suspected its length, very few among us would have had the courage to enter it.

THEOLOGY LOST

The young philosopher whom the Sorbonne had left free to choose his own philosophy thus found himself confronted with the same confusion regarding theology, except that he had not the same liberty. What the self-appointed spokesmen of orthodoxy were saying was mixed up with too many temporal interests to inspire complete confidence, but since every time a priest would try to speak differently he was penalized for it, not always however without some guilt on his part, we did not know which way to turn.

The situation was all the more upsetting because, among the laity, ignorance of sacred doctrine was quite complete. The young Catholics of those days had a very good knowledge of their religion, and while this was most important knowledge, it was also all they knew. Now if to know one's religion is all the knowledge needed for salvation, such knowledge does not confer the competence necessary for understanding and judging theological controversies in which the doctrinal decisions of the Church are under discussion or at stake.

Today the danger is different. To be sure there is no lack of laymen with a smattering of theology who speak as if they were Fathers of the Church. But in the days to which I am referring every young philosopher fresh from his university would feel perfectly qualified in this respect. An *agrégé de philosophie*, if he knew his catechism, felt capable of settling any theological problem whatever. The history of the philosophy taught by Catholic masters in modern French universities may some day be written. The most salient feature of this history will no doubt be that, of so many Catholic philosophers—Lachelier, Delbos, Blondel, and many others —not a single one ever studied theology or felt any scruple about it.

The fact is curious in itself, since the respect for competence is traditional in universities. Their almost excessive confidence in diplomas has no other source. None of us had ever taken a course in theology, we were ignorant of its history, and we had no conception of a theological commentary on Scripture done by a qualified teacher addressing himself to students already past masters in biblical studies. More important still, we were wholly innocent of that theological spirit which, like the legal spirit, can be acquired only by engaging in the practice of the scholastic method under some qualified guide. Nothing later can make up for this lack of an introductory training in theology under the leadership of a master. The lack was there, however, and, what is worse, we were not aware of it. I shall not say that these young laymen lived under the delusion that they knew theology; they did not even suspect that there was something there for them to know. Among our masters, I suppose that Victor Delbos, chiefly trained in Spinoza and Kant, found in the later study of Malebranche his first introduction to theology properly so-called. As for us their pupils, we had no doubt that, if he was a Catholic, a philosopher was thereby a theologian. That is why so many people dabbled in theology in an amateurish way without being aware of incurring any risk. A case in point was a most devout Christian, capable of holding both a chair of philosophy and a chair of mathematics, who did not hesitate to expound the most intricate theological problems. He even undertook to explain to the Church the nature of religious dogmas, as though she had not been promulgating them for centuries. His ignorance of theology was as complete as ours. Doctrinal condemnations were to be expected, but when they came, they took that small world by surprise. Those condemned simply considered themselves persecuted by backward theologians.

It must be said, moreover, that a change had taken place in the teaching of religion, in France at least, and this change was bound to bring about such accidents. What took place at the time can be summed up by saying that modern theologians were stressing more and more the importance of philosophy. Whereas the theologians of the middle ages, following the tradition of the Fathers of the Church, had often denounced the shortcomings of philosophy, their modern successors tended to insist on its necessity. But more about this later. My present point is that to the extent that theology philosophizes, philosophy feels invited to theologize. Now for reasons tied up with the general mentality of our times, the teaching of religious knowledge had tended, and is still tending, to make a maximum use of philosophical reasoning in apologetics. The fact can be confirmed by what has happened to the teaching of the catechism in French parishes between 1900 and 1950. In 1900 French children learned their catechism; they knew it by heart and never forgot it thereafter. Priests were not then as much concerned as they are today about what the children really understood of the catechism. They were taught with a view to the future, to the time when they would be old enough to understand it. To this day, when any hesitation on the true teaching of the Church on a certain point of doctrine occurs to someone so instructed, he always knows to what chapter in his catechism he should turn for an answer. Charles Péguy is a striking example of a French Christian whose religion always remained that of his catechism. It was nothing less and, let us not forget, nothing more. The pastor of the parish church of Saint Aignan in Orléans did a very good job of it. He simply gave Péguy to the Church.

The catechism then taught was admirable in its precision and conciseness. But things have become different. This capsule theology contained all that was required to meet the needs of a whole life. Yielding to the illusion that it was democratic to treat citizens as morons, they brought the catechism down to the level of the masses instead of raising the masses to its level. Hence the low-calorie diet that children are today fed under the name of catechism. Such a practice forgets that the catechism they are taught as children must serve them well beyond their early years. For nine out of ten among them, the religious truth they learn from their first catechism will have to do for the rest of their lives. It should be a substantial food. One never knows whether there is not a future Charles Péguy among the children in a catechism class. One of them may be a Little Flower, a future Doctor of the Church. It is not exaggeration to say that instruction in the catechism is the most important teaching a Christian will ever receive throughout his life, however long or learned it may be. This instruction should therefore carry from the very beginning the maximum of religious knowledge it is able to bear.

The catechism of my youth aimed at nothing else. Knowing that the Christian lives by faith, and anxious to start the child as early as possible on the road to salvation, a concern that is the proper object of religious teaching, our catechism at once placed in our hands the truth of faith, the only truth that saves. This teaching was very far from belittling the resources of reason, but reason always came second after faith, the only knowledge that reaches the God of religion, the God Who saves. It is true that reason can demonstrate there is a God, but when Aristotle for the first time demonstrated the existence of a First Unmoved Mover, he had not yet taken a single step on the path to salvation. All the philosophical demonstrations of God put together will never yield an atom of faith, and since "without faith it is impossible to please God," no certitude coming from my own reason can replace my assent to the truth of revelation. When God tells me of His own existence and bids me to believe His word, He is offering me a share in the knowledge that He has of Himself. This is more than a matter of information; it is an invitation.

The act of faith accepts this invitation, and that is why such an act is properly a religious one, constituting by its very essence an assent to the supernatural and divine truth of which faith is in man a finite but real participation, the beginning of the possession of God's eternal beatitude. Reason is enough for man to know there is a God, but faith is necessary for man to approach God. Besides this is the formal teaching of Scripture (Heb. 11:6): *Accedentem ad Deum oportet credere quia est, et quod inquirentibus se, remunerator sit: For he that cometh to God, must believe that He is: and is a rewarder to them that seek Him.* To let the God of the philosophers and of the scholars take precedence over the God of Abraham, Isaac, and Jacob is to effect a substitution whose consequences can be all the more serious because it takes place in minds that may well never become those of scholars and philosophers.

What Scripture teaches is also what the old catechism used to teach. As an instance of this I shall quote the Catechism of the Diocese of Meaux, in its edition of 1885:

What is the first truth we must believe?
The first truth we must believe is that there is a God and there can be only one.

Why do you believe that there is a God?
I believe that there is a God because He Himself has revealed His existence to us.

Does not reason likewise tell you also that there is a God?
Yes, reason tells us there is a God because, if there were
no God, heaven and earth would not exist.

Let us keep in mind these clear-cut and straightfor-
ward positions. *Credo in unum Deum:* the existence
of God is here given as an object of faith included in the
first article of the Apostles' Creed; it is an object of
faith inasmuch as it was revealed by the word of God
Himself in Scripture. Lastly, following on this point the
teaching of Saint Paul (Rom. 1:20), the catechism
adds that reason *likewise* says there is a God, cause of
the existence of heaven and earth. Such are, in their
terms and sequence, the three fundamental questions
and answers that used to be taught to a child by catechism at its elementary level.

The children of this child, now grown up, have been
taught perceptibly different things. In the catechism
published in 1923 for the Diocese of Paris, a long article
of five questions is devoted to the existence of God.
Instead of asking first why we must *believe* there is a
God, and answering that we believe it on the strength
of His own word, this later catechism asks whether we
are able "to know God with certainty." The answer is,
yes, "since all creatures prove to us His existence." Indeed, creatures can be causes neither of their existence
nor of their order. Hence a creator was necessary to
give them their being, and to establish them in harmony. Another argument is drawn from moral conscience, which supposes a master prescribing good and
forbidding evil. A third reason can be found in universal

consent, for "at all times and in all places people have believed in the existence of God." At the end, the catechism asks whether God has Himself manifested His existence. Answer: "Yes, God Himself has manifested His existence when He revealed Himself to the first human beings, to Moses and to the prophets, and especially in the person of His Son Jesus Christ."

The doctrine remains the same, the order has become different. The God of rational knowledge, Whose existence can be attained by various philosophical ways, is now taking precedence over the God of revelation. In the old days, we first believed that God Himself had spoken to us and then we went on to assure ourselves rationally that indeed there is a God; in 1923, the first thing we did was to make sure that the existence of God can be known "with certainty" by diverse arguments drawn from reason alone: only then did we appeal to God's own testimony. We even went a step further. In the catechism of 1923, the act of faith in the word of God appeared perhaps a bit late, but it did come in the end; it does not enter at all, even at the end, in the elementary catechism French children are taught today. True, the *Illustrated Elementary Catechism* published in Tours in 1949 begins by affirming: "I believe in God"; but it presently gives the reason for this belief, and the reason is not that God Himself has revealed us *His* existence, that is, His own personal existence; no, "I believe in God because nothing can make itself."

What a decline since the catechism of 1885! If it is because nothing can cause itself to be that we believe in God's existence, then we do not *believe* it, we *know* it. *Ex nihilo nihil* is not an object of faith but a philosophical proposition. It even is a proposition borrowed from Lucretius, an Epicurean materialist who directly inferred from it that nothing could be created or annihilated, so much so that the world has always existed and always will. To extract a proof of the existence of God from the negation of the very possibility of creation, it is necessary to introduce a supplementary notion between the principle and the conclusion. There is one indeed and it is that *the world has been made.* Assuredly, if one agrees that the world has been made, only God could have made it, but it is not immediately evident that the world has been made; it is a philosophical conclusion to be demonstrated and the demonstration of creation is possible only on the basis of a certain notion of the existence and the nature of God which requires a prior philosophical discussion. In the *Summa Contra Gentiles* of Thomas Aquinas, the proof of the existence of God comes in Book I, that of the creation of the world follows later in Book II. At any rate, the implications of the problem are becoming rather complicated for young children to unravel.

Let us return to our "illustrated" catechism. When we decide to appeal to reason before appealing to faith, we should not put under the eyes of children a set of images attended by commentaries. Here is a house. Did the house make itself? No. Did this locomotive, this airplane, and this watch make themselves? No, and the answer is correct; but the catechism goes on to say: "The heavens and the stars, the sea with its fishes, the earth with its mountains, its fields, its meadows, its trees, its flowers, its animals cannot have made themselves." And, to repeat, this also is true, with this reservation, however, that they have not made themselves *if they have been made.* Since the catechism adds the precision that "in the beginning there was nothing," what is at stake is really the creation of the world, the production of its whole substance and existence. But then the problem is entirely different from that of the building of a house by an architect, a contractor, and a more or less large number of workmen. Images showing man-fabricated products such as a watch, an engine, or an airplane, are liable to be misleading when the creation of the world *ex nihilo* is at stake. Is there not some danger in getting the child used to thinking that he is in possession of an unshakable rational evidence when, in fact, his conclusion rests upon a pseudophilosophical and worthless argument? To be sure, the creation of the world by God can be philosophically demonstrated; Thomas Aquinas has effectively demonstrated it, but his demonstration has little to do with the making of clocks or the building of houses, and there is really little hope that we can make children understand the meaning of his demonstrations.

I would not waste time in justifying my remarks if I did not know quite well how they will be construed. Some theologians find it hard to distinguish between the abstract order of doctrinal definition and the empirical order of psychological life. Unlike their master Saint Thomas Aquinas, they do not distinguish between the proposition: *there are rational demonstrations of the existence of God,* and the quite different proposition: *all men, in all ages and under all conditions, are able to understand philosophical demonstrations of the existence of God.* This is the proper time to remember the wise remark made by Gabriel Marcel, that the less one stands in need of proofs of the existence of God the easier it is for him to find them. The order to be followed in the religious education of the child is of paramount importance here. Let us leave aside the problem of knowing whether the philosophical God demonstrated by reason is identically the religious God of salvation in Whom Christians believe. It is still a fact, according to Thomas Aquinas himself, that the certitude of faith, which rests on the infallibility of God, is more unshakable than the evidence of the first principles of human reason. If I believe in the existence of God nothing untoward will happen on the day when some unbeliever will question the validity of my proofs. My religious life is not founded on the conclusions of any philosopher: *fundatus sum supra firmam petram*. But if I have first been taught to hold that God exists on the strength of demonstrative reasoning, and only later to believe it, it is to be feared that the reverse will happen. To believe and to believe that one knows are two entirely different things. In the second case, faith seems easy as long as it plays no other part than to support knowledge; but if knowledge loses confidence in itself, then a faith of this sort is liable to be swept away with it. The man who thinks he knows that God exists and then realizes that he no longer knows it also realizes that he no longer believes it.

It is both possible and legitimate to appeal to the common belief in the existence of God natural to mankind. But this is a mere fact; it is neither a matter of religious faith nor a philosophical argument. If we wish to convince the human reason, we should not be willing to offer it metaphysical trash. Should it be objected that metaphysics is too difficult for children, no one will deny it. Metaphysics is difficult for everyone, and this precisely is the reason why, according to Saint Thomas, it was necessary that even the naturally knowable truths required for salvation should be revealed. It was, Saint Thomas says, *necessarium*. Among theologians, those who consider themselves better "Thomists" than Saint Thomas think it advisable to specify that this is only morally necessary: *moraliter necessarium*. Granted, but though of a different order, moral necessity is no less necessary than metaphysical necessity. Thomas Aquinas saw no point in introducing the distinction. In his own perspective, which is that of the salvation of *mankind* in general, the distinction is vain. The will of God was not to make human salvation possible in theory only, but in practice as well. From this point of view, little would have been gained by making such a demonstrative truth theoretically accessible to men if, in fact, an exceedingly small number of them would have been able to understand the demonstration. How many? *Paucissimi*, says Saint Thomas. Hence the advice given by him to each and every one, young and not so young, to receive the truth of God through faith pending the time they will be able to understand it. This was very wise, but it was in the thirteenth century. It would seem that since then we have discovered the art of turning out ten-year-old metaphysicians.

I owe it to the priests who taught me my religion to say that they never watered it down with pseudophilosophy: "I believe in God because He Himself has revealed His existence to us." When they read these words again sixty years later, those who learned to recite them by heart at the time of their youth experience the pleasant feeling of a homecoming. Every one of those truths is as true today as it ever was, and of the same truth. I never had to unlearn a single line of this catechism of 1885, so solid, so full, so firmly grounded in a faith that was friendly to intelligence but aware of being higher in dignity; more important still, I never found in it any occasion of doubt. Let us hope that the Christians of the future will be in a position to say the same thing of the catechism they are learning today.

This tendency to stress the importance of reason is more easily understood when its origin is known. The end of the nineteenth century and the beginning of the twentieth have witnessed the rise of a particular kind of apologetics and one that was quite new when compared with its predecessors. It was a reaction against the traditionalism of the nineteenth century, itself an answer to the anti-religious philosophism of the eighteenth. In his article "Eclecticism" in the *Encyclopedia*, Diderot had set the tone for the freethinkers of the future. His hero was the man who, "trampling on prejudices, tradition, antiquity, universal consent, authority, in short all that which subjugates the common mind, dares to think by himself." Bending before the violence of the attack, many Christians then made the mistake of fighting on the battleground chosen by their adversaries. These had set up reason against faith and religion; therefore, so they thought, reason was their enemy. They could think of no better rejoinder than, in turn, to pitch faith and revelation against reason. Since one had to choose between being a philosopher and being a Christian, one would choose being a Christian against the philosophers. Thus were born a variety of doctrines, linked together by this common spirit of reaction against philosophical reason. Such were those of De Bonald, La Mennais, Bonnetty, Bautain, and others. The most representative among them was the eloquent and popular Theatine preacher Ventura de Raulica.

This Italian monk, who preached in French with convincing zeal, gave in 1851 a series of sermons entitled *Philosophical Reason and Catholic Reason*. The title alone says enough. Grounded on faith and tradition, "Catholic reason" is good. On the contrary, philosophical reason is evil because it considers itself "by that which it is and can naturally do, without the assistance of a reason other and higher than itself, as able to acquire by reasoning all essential truths, either speculative or ethical." To the philosophical reason of ancient times "abject in its origin, absurd in its method, un-

happy in its results, evil in its consequences," the eloquent Theatine opposed "Catholic reason, which alone
is fortunate enough to avoid error, to possess truth, because it is based first and foremost on the teaching and
the doctrines of Jesus Christ."

It is in the perspective of such traditionalisms, almost
all of which have been censured in Rome, that we
should read the decision of the Vatican Council on the
possibility of knowing the existence of God by the sole
light of the natural reason. At that very moment, the
pendulum began again to swing in the opposite direction. In his collected sermons of 1851, Ventura de
Raulica had quoted in support of his own opinions a
rather curious letter addressed by the Bishop of Mon-
tauban to Augustin Bonnetty, director of the *Annales
de philosophie chrétienne*. Among other things, the
Bishop said: "We are granting to reason more than its
due if we attribute to it the knowledge of God by way
of demonstration." The Vatican Council, in other words,
restored to the natural reason its proper rights and
solemnly confirmed its power to attain a rationally demonstrated knowledge of God.

This was the history of a generation prior to ours and,
in the time of our youth, we knew nothing of it. Hence
our surprise to find ourselves confronted, within the
Church, with a school of philosophers for whose existence we could not in any way account. We did not
know that they represented a rationalist reaction against
the answer of traditionalism to the challenge of eight-
eenth-century philosophism. Naturally we were aston-
ished to meet Christian teachers who made it a point
not to *believe* in the existence of God or in any conclusion of natural theology demonstrable by the light
of human reason such as those that theologians, with
Thomas Aquinas, call "preambles to faith." Thus, in the

face of all that which the traditionalists had considered inaccessible to reason unaided by revelation and faith, this new school of theologians maintained, on the contrary, not only that the reason is by itself capable of knowing it, but even that we cannot know it in any other way.

This attitude was all the more bewildering because essentially religious motives were at its origin. It was a sort of apologetic rationalism. In those early years of the twentieth century, when science was supreme and nothing was respected that was not strictly scientific, it is understandable that zealous priests should have resented the discredit in which Catholic writings were held by so many unbelievers. By setting faith aside, they were hoping to attract the attention and gain the respect of the non-Catholic scientists and philosophers. The history of their endeavor to sever philosophy from theology has not yet been studied as it deserves to be. Not that they wanted to achieve this separation as the Averroists of the thirteenth century had done, by despairing of bridging the gap between their philosophy and their religion; on the contrary, it was their ambition to show forth the perfect agreement spontaneously achieved between religion and philosophy by a reason that was wholly independent of faith.

These masters were justified in stressing the power of the natural reason to know such truths as the existence of God, His oneness, and the like, without resorting to the light of revelation. It is more difficult to understand why, following the pendulum to the end of its swing, they deemed it necessary to posit as impossible an act of religious faith in the existence of God. Still, this is precisely what they did. In 1925, in the seventh edition of an elementary treatise on philosophy for use in Catholic schools, one could read this remarkable proposition: "The existence of God cannot be the object of an act of divine faith." One could well be surprised. The Vatican Council had taught that the reason was capable of knowing by itself and with certainty that God exists, that is to say, of demonstrating His existence. But that Council did not forbid belief in the existence of God nor did it declare that such an act of faith was impossible.

The incident was in itself of no importance. It deserves to be mentioned here only because it is witness to a state of mind that was rather widespread in those days and that has not completely disappeared in our own day. Such a state of mind suggests that men should be taught the proofs of the existence of God rather than be invited to take at their face value the words of their daily prayers: "I believe in God, Father almighty . . ." For indeed how could they believe in Him without believing that He exists? It is not difficult for us to see how these diverse attitudes are linked together when we read in the same philosophy textbook written for Catholic schools that at first revelation was "morally necessary" to mankind to preserve its patrimony of speculative and moral truths, but that it is not "physically" necessary, all the more so as to believe in some of these revealed tenets has become impossible. Here are young Christians convinced that, even if they wanted to do so, they could not believe in the existence of God. Were it not for the priceless aptitude of students not to take seriously everything that their professors say, one would feel frightened at the thought that such opinions could have been conceived, written, and taught in some Christian schools at the beginning of the twentieth century.

The most remarkable aspect about this doctrine is that it did not provoke any protestations. This was fortunate, since it is a waste of time to discuss propositions which the lives of their authors eloquently contradict. There was neither philosophism nor rationalism behind the words of these Christian teachers. Quite the contrary, the greatest glory of God was the only motive of those who spoke in that way. In speaking as pure philosophers and without appealing to faith, they hoped to persuade unbelievers to consider seriously the philosophical teaching given in Christian schools. Unbelievers are not simple enough not to detect the presence of a religious concern under this apparent rationalism. Besides, one should not forget that outside the Catholic Church there are other people besides unbelievers. The only theologian who resented this attitude was a Calvinist. In his book *On the Nature of Religious Knowledge,* published in Paris in 1931, A. Lecerf denounced a doctrine that perfectly embodied what Catholicism should be in order to justify the attacks of Protestants. A. Lecerf was no Barthian. This Calvinist harbored no hostility against the natural reason even such as it has been since the Fall. He was simply a Christian who believed in the essential distinction there is between the order of nature and the order of grace. This is the reason why this Calvinist theologian maintained that natural theology, that is, metaphysics, is "incapable of founding *religious* knowledge." In this view he was entirely right and he showed himself faithful to Catholic truth. Metaphysics can open *preambles* to faith, only the Word of God can *found* it.

Christian philosophers were shocked by such doctrines, but their faith was not shaken. No one could persuade them that it was "physically" impossible to make an act of faith in the existence of God. They were making one several times a day, they even sang it at high Mass on Sundays; above all, still remembering their catechism of 1885, they would say: "I believe there is a God because He Himself has revealed His existence to us." Besides, it is theologically true to say that the assent of intellect and will to the word of God revealing to us, not the existence of *a* God, but His very own existence, is the indispensable foundation of a properly religious knowledge. If there are Calvinists who believe that the teaching of the Catholic Church forbids them to subscribe to this truth, ill-informed teachers may well be responsible for their illusion, but it is nonetheless an illusion. Faith in God implies all the knowledge necessary for salvation including that of God's existence. At all times, since the beginning of the world, Saint Thomas says in the *De Veritate* (14, 11), every man has been required to believe explicitly that God exists and provides for the needs of men.

It is all the more remarkable that this fundamental religious truth finds so little acceptance in the minds of Christian philosophers today, let alone theologians. In the thirteenth century the main effort of theology had been to stress the necessity of faith and the insufficiency of the philosophical reason to bring about the salvation of man. Besides, this was the point the Church asked them to enforce. Let them not pretend they are philosophers! *Nec philosophos se ostentent* . . . these were the words of Pope Gregory IX speaking in 1231 of the theologians of the University of Paris. Today, some of our teachers are still willing enough to be theologians, but not everywhere nor at all times, even when the knowledge of God is at stake. It is not enough for some of them to say that natural theology is possible and even highly useful, which nobody denies—they make it compulsory. Fideism is the natural temptation of Protestantism; a certain unconscious rationalism has regularly been the danger tempting our Catholic theologians. Read the admonitions of Pope Gregory IX, read his pressing injunctions to the Parisian masters of the thirteenth century, and you will realize that this state of mind is not a particularly recent one. Nevertheless it was certainly alive in 1936, and *Christianity and Philosophy* was expressly written to oppose it.

As was to be expected, objections were not lacking. Father Lucien Laberthonnière criticized the book for still granting to philosophy too much independence from religion. This was to be expected. The director of the *Annales de philosophie chrétienne* was thus keeping faith with the tradition of this ancient journal. In his view, merely to distinguish these two disciplines was to fall into an exaggerated separation. But the objections came more from the side of reason than of faith. Not a single objection took any account of the text of the Epistle to the Hebrews, or of the explanation that Thomas Aquinas gave of it, although the thesis in question rested upon them. Laymen or clerics, not one of those who argued against the book was in the least interested in its scriptural and theological justification. Indeed, since these Christians were upholding the rights of philosophy, it was to be expected that their arguments should be derived not from scriptural texts but from reason.

The objections had in common another feature, namely, a kind of radical (*in radice*) inability to discern the religious meaning of the problem.

For philosophers, even Christian ones, the whole thing boils down to a problem of information. Let us imagine a theology one mile long; the question for them is to know how many yards of it can be covered by reason alone, while the rest of the distance belongs by right to faith. But in reality things are not that way. When the theologian accompanies the philosopher with sympathetic vigilance to know how far the natural reason will go, he himself has already reached the goal. Indeed what to the theologian is a starting point will remain for philosophers in this life a but partially accessible goal. However obscurely, faith already possesses the very substance of all that philosophy will ever know about God, and even more. But faith possesses it in a different way, that is, as a theological virtue which is in itself a participation in the divine life and a token of the beatific vision. This distinction of orders allows us to understand how the same intellect can know by reason the God of philosophy and know by faith the God of Moses, of Abraham, of Isaac, and of Jacob. This is not for the intellect to know and to believe the same thing at the same time and in the same way. For philosophy knows nothing of the God of Scripture. Philosophy knows that there exists a being that all call God, but no philosophy can suspect the existence of the God of Scripture. This is why, exclusively interested in the knowledge that saves, the theologian will always lead the philosopher back to his own starting point: *Accedentem ad Deum oportet credere quia est* . . . Not only do we need the Christian revelation to believe in the God of the Christian religion, but it is senseless to imagine that His existence could be known otherwise than through faith in His own revelation.

A third mark of the state of mind that dictated these objections is more delicate to formulate, but it is so important that I will chance it. It is, let us say, the slightly suspicious nature of the rationalist zeal. Whether priest or layman, theologian or philosopher, the Christian who defends against you the rights of reason will soon accuse you of heresy. It is inevitable as well as so convenient! Here is a man who took the trouble to write a book, no doubt because he thinks that he has something to say, but what he says impresses us as being unusual. So we begin by attributing to him "a very particular conception of the relations of philosophy and theology," *particular* because it is not ours. It then remains for us to get rid of it. This is done by attributing to him such a patently absurd thesis that it needs no refutation. In the present case, he will be accused of refusing the name *philosopher* to all who do not place philosophy in the service of Christian revelation. This absurdity usefully replaces the position of the misunderstood author. And now to kill the thing off. This author who criticizes Luther and Calvin "is in his own interpretation much closer to them than he believes . . . Actually Mr. Gilson is ill protected against a certain masked Jansenism which remains so powerful in French Catholicism: his true adversary is not so much the Reformation as the Renaissance which he has condemned wholesale for putting too much trust in the human reason." Let us stop here, for at this point, combining classroom dialectic with what is worst in theological denunciations, our critic cannot fail to score.

Still, I never condemned the Renaissance wholesale, neither there nor anywhere else. But I did condemn the naturalism of the Renaissance, which is an altogether different thing. What interests me most is that, instead of taking into account the precise texts from Scripture and Saint Thomas on which the thesis that he dislikes is based, my critic finds in it an aftertaste of Lutheranism, Calvinism, and Jansenism. This does not surprise me, and indeed I am used to it. To replace a refutation with an accusation of heresy is good warfare. Still, philosophers should refrain from using this theological weapon. Above all, they should not appeal to the re-

ligious faith of their adversary to make him do justice
to the sufficiency of reason.

Such is however the distinctive characteristic of this
pseudorationalism. The trust that the most rationalist
of theologians puts in the natural light of man will never
make him omit a final appeal to the supreme authority
of the Church. His rationalism is always backed up by
a Council.

Twice in my life I had this memorable experience.
The first time was in Europe in the course of a meeting
of Catholic philosophers including laymen and priests;
the second time at a meeting of students and teachers
in a Catholic college of the United States. Both times I
purposely ventured to express these two remarks which
I knew would bring opposition: *All that which is in the*
Summa Theologiae *is theology; I believe in the existence
of God.* Both times the reaction was instantaneous and
identical: I was a fideist. This was proved to me on the
spot by quoting the *Constitutio Dogmatica de Fide
Catholica* of the Vatican Council, decision of April 24,
1870. Had it been at hand, my opponents might as well
have quoted the formula found in the *Motu Proprio*
of Pius X, *Sacrorum Antistitum,* September 1, 1910:
"God as beginning and end of all things, can be known
with certainty and even demonstrated by the natural
light of the reason from the things that have been made,
that is, the visible works of creation, even as the cause
is known by its effects." I protested in vain that I believed all this and even knew it so well I had no need to
believe it; I could not make myself understood. They
would repeatedly answer me: If you would truly admit
a demonstration of the existence of God, not only would
you not need to believe it, but you could not.

What disorder! But we do not want to enter that

maze. These anecdotes are reported here to one purpose only, which is to make more tangible the shape of
a certain brand of rationalism that is so exacting toward
others and so indulgent toward itself. The decision of
the Vatican Council and the words of Pius X upholding
the power of the natural reason are based on a well-
known text of Saint Paul (Rom. 1:20). These doctrinal
acts of the Church are essentially religious acts; the
Church is fully entitled to make such decisions and she
has authority to promulgate them. Theologians are
therefore justified in appealing to the authority of the
Church to make a Christian admit that reason unaided
by faith can demonstrate the existence of God. Still,
this appeal to the authority of the Councils addresses
itself to religious faith, not to reason. It is a theological
justification of the internal sufficiency of the reason.
Moreover, there is a vast difference between saying that
the existence of God is rationally demonstrable and saying that it cannot be believed. In fact, according to
Thomas Aquinas, this truth is both believable and
demonstrable. But who among us then knew anything
about the theology of Saint Thomas Aquinas? History
was to be for us the means to discover it.

THEOLOGY REGAINED

Clio alone made it possible for us to bring some order to this confusion by unraveling its origins. But she could not do it without calling into question several accepted historical attitudes. Attitudes of this sort are the harder to modify, as they are taken for granted.

A first one is well enough described by Victor Cousin at the beginning of his *Cours de philosophie* of 1818: "There are only two really distinct periods in the history of philosophy as well as in the history of the world: Antiquity and Modern Times." Between the two the light of the Greek genius "gradually fades away into the night of the Middle Ages." The fifteenth and the sixteenth centuries are nothing else than the begetting of the seventeenth century. In short, "the second period begins with Descartes." Cousin did not intend to express an official view of history; this was to him an evidence not to be questioned. In 1905 Octave Hamelin was still writing that, in philosophy proper, Descartes came after the ancients almost as though nothing had taken place between them and himself. There was first a Greek philosophy, then a modern philosophy came; between these two, nothing, except perhaps a theology based on faith and authority, which are the very negation of philosophy. In 1905 my master Lucien Lévy-Bruhl, one of the men to whom I owe a very great debt of gratitude, suggested to me as a subject for research work: Descartes and scholasticism. In doing so, he had in mind the well-known essay of Freudenthal, *Spinoza and Scholasticism*. I knew nothing of scholasticism. I had not read a single line of Saint Thomas Aquinas and no professor had ever taught me his doctrine; but Lucien Lévy-Bruhl knew I was a Catholic and on this basis he inferred that the reverse was true. So it was to gratify me that this subject was suggested to me by the sociologist who had written *Primitive Mentality*. Let this detail be noted in support of the perfect testimony of Charles Péguy on "that kind of great liberality, generosity of mind and even of heart which philosophy had in the teaching of our master." The "goodness of heart of that philosophical teaching": it was exactly that; it could not be said better.

The 1913 thesis on *Freedom in Descartes and Theology* was born of this research. The conclusions were surprising to me. It was on the occasion of this work that, having to go back from Descartes to what I supposed to be the medieval sources of his philosophy, I became acquainted for the first time with Saint Thomas Aquinas and other scholastic theologians. A surprising number of notions and conclusions had passed from their doctrines into that of Descartes, but the word "source" does not adequately describe the situation. Nothing really "flows" from scholastic theology into Cartesian philosophy. Descartes had not come from scholasticism as from a source, he had exploited it as a quarry. As the work progressed, I experienced a growing feeling of intellectual dismay in seeing what impoverishment metaphysics had suffered at the hands of Descartes. Most of the philosophical positions he had retained had their proper justification, not in his own works, but in those of the scholastics. Nor were the conclusions of Descartes' doctrine at stake; what made me uneasy was the casual way in which Descartes retained conclusions without going to the trouble of establishing them. From scholasticism to Cartesianism the loss in metaphysical substance seemed to me frightening. Looking back across forty-five years I distinctly remember the feeling of fear I experienced on the day when, after holding back my pen for a long time, I finally wrote this simple sentence: "On all these points the thought of Descartes, in comparison with the sources from which it derives, marks much less a gain than a loss." Since this appeared to me to be true, I had to say it, but in so doing I was violating a canon. This conclusion questioned historical views so commonly received that they were almost dogmas. If it is possible to find in the middle ages metaphysical conclusions better worked out technically and more completely justified than they are in Descartes, then it becomes difficult to maintain with Cousin that between the Greeks and Descartes there was nothing but a progressive dimming of the Greek light leading to a sort of intellectual night. If on certain points there is more in Saint Thomas than in Descartes, one can no longer say with Hamelin that "Descartes appears after the ancients as though there was nothing between the Greeks and himself."

This change in historical perspective was fraught with a properly philosophical problem. Victor Cousin had made elsewhere this perfectly correct remark: "The philosophy that had preceded Descartes was theology." Since at the time when Cousin wrote these lines the philosophy of Descartes was considered essentially a rejection of scholasticism, the situation was simple: first Saint Thomas, then Descartes; first theology, then philosophy. But if I was right in saying that Descartes had borrowed materials from Saint Thomas, the situation was becoming much less simple. Under this new perspective, what had been theology in scholasticism had become philosophy in Cartesianism. Hence, there could not be between philosophy and theology the opposition in essence so much talked about in our own times. More exactly still, Descartes could not have extracted so much philosophy from scholasticism if, under one form or another, philosophy had not been present in it. I had to conclude, therefore, that there had been philosophy in the middle ages. The next step was to go back there and to look for it.

A last problem still had to be solved. It was too early for me to attempt to solve it, but I realized that I could not forget it. This philosophy that Descartes had found in scholasticism, how did it get there? Through Greece, no doubt, and especially owing to Aristotle; but Aristotle happened to be precisely what Descartes detested in scholasticism, the Christian conclusions of which were the only points he retained. The existence of a unique God, infinite, simple, supremely free, Creator of the universe as an all-powerful efficient cause, and of man himself, made to His image and likeness, endowed with an immaterial soul capable of surviving its body—not one of these notions could be found in Aristotle. But they all were easy to find in any scholastic theologian and Descartes inherited all of them. It is therefore a fact that Greek philosophy came out of the middle ages other than it had been in the minds of the ancient philosophers. On every one of these points Descartes came after the middle ages almost as if the Greeks had never existed. Now since it is owing to Christian theology that philosophy had undergone this deep transformation, theology has not merely contained a metaphysics, it must have had the capacity to produce the very metaphysical conclusions that Descartes inherited from the middle ages. This double transformation, first of Greek philosophy into Christian theology, then of Christian theology into modern philosophy, agreed badly with the opposition traditionally recognized between the two disciplines. It thus became all the more necessary to go back to that ancient philosophy of the theologians in order to examine its nature and to assess it.

The awareness of this necessity led me to undertake a serious study of Thomas Aquinas. In particular, I thought I should study him in his theological writings, since these were the only ones in which could be found, in its organic unity, the body of doctrine that became, by way of Descartes, the common patrimony of modern philosophy in the seventeenth century. Hence the modest course of lectures, *Le Thomisme,* first given at the University of Lille in 1913–14, and which, because it found no publisher in Paris, was published in Strasbourg in 1919. The book deserves to survive in this first edition as a monument to the ignorance of its author. Incidentally, as an almost complete collection of all the misprints imaginable, it is a typographical curiosity.

Of the criticisms directed against the book, three have remained in my memory. One of them, very much to the point, originated with Maurice de Wulf. He criticized the book for the all too real weakness of its properly metaphysical part. I resolved at the time to take his remarks into account and I hope that I have since done it. The second objection was that I had followed a theological order in expounding the philosophical doctrine of Saint Thomas. More about this later. The third reproach came from a theologian of the Catholic University of Toulouse who wondered how I could speak of a "philosophy of Saint Thomas," since Saint Thomas had had no philosophy of his own but had simply shared with his contemporaries the common philosophy of the day? In other words, this critic gave me to understand that I could have expounded the so-called philosophy of Saint Thomas from the writings of any one of the scholastic theologians of the thirteenth century as well as from his own. My critic, I imagine, recognized with the historian Maurice de Wulf the existence of a "scholastic synthesis," consisting chiefly of the philosophical technique of Aristotle, adopted by all the scholastics as a sort of "common good."

The origin of this historical point of view is easily explained. The same Christian teachers who, for the reasons explained above, desired to establish in our own day a philosophy entirely independent of theology, were simply projecting into the past their doctrinal ideal. Anxious not to lose contact with their own tradition, these teachers adapted it to their own needs: they constructed a medieval philosophy as completely independent of all theology as their own aimed to be. There is no useless effort in history; no historian can record of the past more than he can see from his own point of view.

The only way to know if the philosophy of Saint Thomas was the same as that of the other scholastics was to compare it with the doctrines of other teachers of the day. Hence the study, *The Philosophy of Saint Bonaventure* published in 1924. The task was made easy because of the excellent edition of the complete works of the saint prepared by the Franciscan Fathers of Quaracchi. The doctrinal expositions of this theologian are so well ordered and so limpid that his historian often needs only to translate the text. The teaching of Saint Bonaventure was visibly different from that of Saint Thomas. The fundamental notions of being, cause, intellect, and natural knowledge were different in the two doctrines. We had therefore at least two medieval philosophies in hand, and everything was running smoothly when Father Mandonnet, O.P., came along and reversed the data of the problem.

A first-rate historian, Father Pierre Mandonnet was also every inch a Dominican and his intellectualism inspired him with a decided hostility, at times almost comical, toward everything Franciscan or favoring affective theology. Confronted with the doctrine of Saint

Bonaventure, O.F.M., in which the Augustinian inspiration is scarcely hidden under the Aristotelian phraseology, the reaction of Father Mandonnet was immediate and vigorous: as a doctrinal exposition the book was acceptable, but its author had chosen the wrong title. There is no philosophy in a doctrine in which the distinction of faith and reason is as vague as it is in that of Saint Bonaventure. The correct title of the book should have been "The Theology of Saint Bonaventure." Father Mandonnet did not intend to deny that the middle ages had been able to conceive a precise notion of philosophy. On the contrary, he maintained that there had certainly been one philosopher and one philosophy worthy of the name, Saint Thomas Aquinas, O.P., and Thomistic philosophy. Saint Thomas had known how to conceive and to apply the distinction between the two disciplines, that is, to think as a theologian in all matters pertaining to theology and as a philosopher in all matters pertaining to philosophy. So the Christian middle ages had had one philosopher, but one only.

Thus, after starting from a middle ages without any philosopher, I had thought for a time that I had found two, but after Father Mandonnet had eliminated Saint Bonaventure, there remained only one. The situation was embarrassing. While one theologian was contending that Saint Thomas had no philosophy of his own, another theologian was asserting to the contrary that the only philosophy to be found in the thirteenth century was that of Saint Thomas Aquinas. This was most unlikely. I myself was quite satisfied that genuine philosophical speculation could be found in Thomas Aquinas; but that there was none in Saint Augustine, John Scotus Erigena, or Saint Anselm, how was I to believe this? Rather, there were grounds to fear that Father Mandonnet's loyalty to the Dominican Order was once more carrying him outside history.

How to get out of this maze? Besides, the situation was becoming somewhat laughable. Let us not forget my point of departure. I had set out to fill in the historical gap between Greek philosophy and modern philosophy. In the beginning, I had foreseen no resistance on the side of the scholastic philosophers. On the contrary, I rather imagined that they would be pleased to find an unexpected ally in their fight for scholasticism. I was mistaken and I began to realize it when Father Mandonnet left me with only Saint Thomas Aquinas to people that vast medieval philosophical wilderness. I had reached this point when another Dominican completed my bewilderment. As much of an intellectualist as his teacher Father Mandonnet, Father Gabriel Théry, O.P., added to this quality a complete indifference to commonly received ideas. He too had no use for poor Roger Bacon, O.F.M., whose very name was enough to irritate Father Mandonnet, but he was unconcerned about accepted historical attitudes even within his own order. Father Théry was the one who finally opened my eyes. Speaking of a new edition of my book *Le Thomisme*, Father Théry simply called my attention to the fact that the doctrine of Saint Bonaventure was indeed a theology, but that the same could be said of the doctrine of Saint Thomas Aquinas. In both cases, I had extracted from their theologies a number of theses, I had then rearranged them so as to make them look like philosophy, and I had dubbed their authors philosophers. In fact, their works were theologies and they themselves were theologians. What I had called their philosophies were "truncated theologies."

This was true. It was even the most immediate evidence conceivable and as soon as it was pointed out to me my mind grasped it eagerly. I had made the typical mistake of a young student in philosophy who, noticing a to him inexplicable lacuna in the teaching of the history of philosophy, resolves to fill it in. I had first made sure of one medieval philosopher, then of two, but Father Mandonnet had taken away the second one; and now Father Théry came along and took away from me the first one. I was again left without medieval philosophies at all; I had only theologies. I had proved that Victor Cousin was right.

There was only one thing I could do. I had to restudy the problem on a serious basis by taking into account all its known data. These were, first, a series of theses on God, the world, and man, which as to their substance could equally have been taught by modern philosophers and by scholastic theologians; second, the surprising fact that the bulk of these theses could be found, expressly formulated, only in the *theological* works of Saint Thomas, Saint Bonaventure, and the rest; last, the puzzling circumstance that not one among these doctors had ever attempted a comprehensive survey of these doctrines presented in a properly philosophical order, that is, ascending to God from His creatures; rather, they had always followed the typically theological order, descending from God to His works. I here have in mind their commentaries on the *Sentences* of Peter Lombard, their Disputed Questions, and their *Summae*, the only writings in which they intended to express their personal thought. The problem then is to find a name that fits a doctrine of this kind, taken with all its distinctive characteristics. There would seem to be only one: *theology*. The main reason so many historians, philosophers, and theologians avoid calling "theology" what they prefer to label "philosophy" is that, in their minds, theology and philosophy are mutually exclusive notions. If we are to believe such thinkers, purely philosophical truths derive entirely from the unaided reason and cannot find a place in theology, in which all conclusions are drawn from faith. Now it is true that all the conclusions of the theologian depend on faith, but it does not follow that they must all be deduced from it. Clearly, it was the true meaning of the word "theology" that stood in need of rediscovery, including the precise conception it implied of the relationship of reason to faith in the mind of a Christian philosopher.

The reader will appreciate my skipping the narrative of the intellectual wanderings which led me out of this confusion. Let me observe, however, that history had led me into this trouble and history helped me to find my way out of it. There had been considerable naïveté in my early decision to apply to the theologians of the middle ages the same method of inquiry that Lucien Lévy-Bruhl and Victor Delbos had taught me to apply to the study of modern philosophers. A problem had evidently escaped my attention. I had assumed that Saint Thomas and Saint Bonaventure were philosophers, which I should have proved before applying to their writings the methods suitable for the history of philosophy. However, there was a good side to this error of perspective. I have always respected the rule laid down by my professors at the Sorbonne, that the history of philosophy does not consist in creating a doctrine and attributing it to a philosopher but, on the contrary, in never ascribing to him anything that it is not reasonably certain he himself thought and said. To refrain from inventing in order to better understand is one of the leading methodological principles in the history of ideas. It was through studying Saint Thomas as though he were a philosopher that I finally had to bow to the evidence that he did not philosophize like other philosophers. This is why I cannot regret that I stood my ground against the combined weight of the critics who were reproaching me with expounding the *philosophy* of Saint Thomas according to a *theological* order. I never gave in on this point. In order to ascribe to Saint Thomas a philosophical mode of exposition, I should have had to make it up. Those who flatter themselves that they can do it begin by simplifying the problem. They first identify the doctrine of Saint Thomas with the doctrine of Aristotle, after which it becomes easy for them to expound it according to the order assigned to philosophy by Aristotle himself. But this is also why so many "Thomists" have missed the deepest meaning of the teaching of their master. Besides, history is not exactly the forte of scholasticism. Deep within themselves, scholastics rather despise and mistrust history. The University practiced it better, and as a result the understanding of the theology of Saint Thomas has greatly benefited from it.

A theology cannot be interpreted as if it were a philosophy; but the way to study in the writings of a theologian what he himself calls theology differs in no way from a correct historical approach to what a philosopher calls philosophy. It finally became necessary for me to examine more closely the notion of what Thomas Aquinas himself calls "theology." The first result of this effort was to dispel a very widespread illusion regarding the true nature of this discipline. It is commonly said that all conclusions whose premises are known in the sole light of the natural reason are by this very fact philosophical. And this is true. But many presently add that since this kind of reasoning is philosophical it has no place in theology. Another way of expressing the same idea is to say that all theological conclusions come at the end of syllogisms one of whose premises is held by faith.

This way of understanding theology is true in that which it affirms but insufficient in what it denies. It is correct to say that the subject matter of supernatural theology is the "revealed," that is to say, truths that can be known to man only through revelation. Now the "revealed" as such can be received only by faith. Hence it is true to say that theological reasoning argues from faith as its starting point and, as a consequence, is valid only for minds that assent to faith. But this is not the whole question. From the fact that a conclusion drawn from faith cannot belong in philosophy, it does not follow that a purely rational conclusion cannot belong in theology. Quite the contrary, it is of the essence of the theology called "scholastic" that it appeals freely and widely to philosophical reasoning. Because it draws on faith, it is a scholastic *theology*, but because of its distinctive use of philosophy, it is a *scholastic* theology. One cannot understand this position without sharing in the lofty notion Saint Thomas had of the absolute transcendence of theological wisdom over all the other disciplines, including natural theology or metaphysics. I beg to emphasize the point. For though the notion at stake may be easy to understand, many will not subscribe to it, and in any case it takes time to get used to it.

Saint Thomas describes sacred knowledge in the first question of the *Summa Theologiae*, but a correct understanding of what he says of it at that place presupposes the knowledge of his later explanation of the nature of faith. It is only in the perspective of faith considered as a theological virtue—that is to say, as a participation in the divine life—that one gives a concrete meaning to the Thomistic notion of theology. Only in this perspective does one understand why it is necessary to set theology apart from the other disciplines in an order that is not simply above theirs but beyond their reach. Theology is not a science superior to the others *in the same order,* it is not a meta-metaphysics. Based on faith, theology finds itself in a continuity of order with the other sciences, but its nature is different because there can be no continuity of essence between the natural and the supernatural. For the same reason, the relation of theology to the other sciences differs in nature from that of the other sciences among themselves. Hence one cannot make inferences from the other sciences to theology with exactitude. For instance, one cannot say that theology is to metaphysics as metaphysics is to physics; the relation is only *analogous.* Indeed, the divine character of the virtue of faith, through which we become participants in God's own knowledge, is precisely that which makes it possible for theology to assimilate elements borrowed from philosophy and the other scientific disciplines without losing its transcendence and the purity of its essence. This is the gist of the problem.

Here is the proper frame of mind in which to approach difficulties well known in schools of scholastic theology. The question can rightly be called famous because it was one of the main issues at the time of the Reformation. In many respects it is still so today. The old name of Luther and the contemporary name of Karl Barth are sufficient evidence of the fact. If, they say, theology is a truly divine science, in which everything is a sharing in the knowledge that God has, or rather is, how can scholastic theologians dare compromise its transcendence by blending it with cognitions accessible to the natural light of the human reason?

The answer to this difficulty is to be taken from the very principle from which it stems. Nothing escapes the knowledge that God has of Himself. In knowing Himself God also knows all that of which He is or can be the cause. Being a human participation of the divine science, and literally an analogue of it, our theology must be able to include within its knowledge of God that of the totality of finite beings inasmuch as it hangs on God as on its cause. Thereby the totality of the sciences is likewise included within it. Theology claims them as its own as being included within its object. Such knowledge of them does not naturalize theology any more than the knowledge that God has of His own works compromises His divinity.

A theology need not necessarily be scholastic, but it can be, and the condition for such a possibility rests on this fundamental position: everything can be included in a theology of this kind without impairing its unity, because "it is in us as an imprint of divine science, law one and simple of all things." Theology then is at the summit of the hierarchy of the sciences, in a manner analogous to the way in which God is the summit of being. As such, theology transcends all the divisions and all the limitations of the disciplines it includes in its unity without confusion. It contains all human science by mode of eminence, to the extent at least to which it deems it advisable to incorporate it within itself and make it serve its own ends.

So be it, one will say, that takes care of theology! But what becomes of philosophy in this venture? Can it be thus used by theology toward ends that are not its own without losing its essence in the process? In a way it does lose its essence, and it profits by the change. The reproach was already made to Saint Thomas. Some theologians charged him with mixing the water of philosophy with the wine of Scripture, but he refuted the argument by a comparison drawn from the very science he was accused of exploiting. In a simple mixture, he said, the component elements retain their respective natures and continue to subsist in the compound, just as wine and water are found in watered wine. But theology is not a compound, it is not composed of heterogeneous elements of which some would be philosophy and the rest Scripture; all in it is homogeneous despite the diversity of origin. "Those who resort to philosophical arguments in Holy Scripture and put them in the service of faith, do not mix water with wine, they change it to wine." Translate: they change philosophy into theology, just as Jesus changed water to wine at the marriage feast in Cana. Thus can theological wisdom, imprinted in the mind of the theologian as the seal of God's knowing, include the totality of human knowledge in its transcendent unity.

Ut sic sacra doctrina sit velut quaedam impressio divinae scientiae. . . . These enlightening words should always be kept in mind while reading Saint Thomas. They contain the answers to the troublesome questions that had ceaselessly assailed my mind, especially this one: how can purely rational speculation be included in theological speculation without corrupting it or being corrupted by it? The answer is that philosophy needs to keep its rationality to be of service to theology, just as theology must preserve its own transcendence if it is to make use of philosophy. The famous formula: *philosophy the handmaid of theology,* has no other meaning. To be of service a handmaid must first exist, and although it is true that the handmaid is not the mistress, she belongs to the household.

When, after years spent in confusion, this true notion of scholastic theology shed its light on the problem, facts fell into place and seemingly inextricable difficulties suddenly vanished. The scholastic theologies of the middle ages were true theologies; none of them was a philosophy. Neither their ultimate problems, nor their methods, nor the light in which they resolved these problems were the same as in philosophy. Nevertheless the theologies of Albert the Great, Bonaventure, Thomas Aquinas, and John Duns Scotus had made original contributions, many of which in time became integral parts of the metaphysics, the epistemology, and the ethics of later philosophies. Since certain theological conclusions of the middle ages thus became philosophical conclusions in the seventeenth century and after, they must have been rational from the beginning. We are gratuitously creating an insoluble difficulty when we substitute for the true notion of scholastic theology— a science, one and universal like that of God—the impoverished notion of it so widespread in our day.

The attitude of Saint Thomas toward philosophy and the philosophers is thereby made clear. In a well-known chapter of his work *Le système du monde,* Pierre Duhem once denounced what he called the incoherence of Thomism. Considered as a mere philosophy, Duhem said, it was but a mosaic, no doubt a clever one, but made of bits and pieces whose incompatibility appeared from that of their respective origins. Pierre Duhem insisted that he was concerned with Thomism purely as a philosophy, not as a theology. But precisely, Thomism is essentially a theology; it is not a philosophy consisting of pieces borrowed from heterogeneous philosophical sources; rather, it is a theology availing itself of the resources of various philosophies because, in Saint Thomas' own words, theology uses the philosophical disciplines at will (*ut vult*). The theology of Saint Thomas includes philosophical notions of diverse origins, *but it does not consist of them.* Theology chooses and perfects these notions; it descries beyond each one of them a converging point toward which they all tend without being aware of it.

None of the doctrines assimilated by Thomas' theology enters it except under the transforming light of faith in the word of God. What the historian of philosophy denounces in Saint Thomas as abusive interpretations of texts in the sense of his own doctrine, are, on the part of the theologian, neither an act of violence nor a misinterpretation, but rather invitations addressed to the philosophers, offers and propositions made to them to exchange their respective partial truths for *the* truth. To facilitate this exchange, Saint Thomas often instills a new meaning in their old formulas; and this is why to read him as a simple philosopher will always rouse perplexities. These seemingly arbitrary meetings of unrelated philosophies that he likes to call should not be mistaken for so many confusions on his part. To be sure, one single philosophy cannot include the philosophies of Aristotle and Averroes, of Plato, Plotinus, and Avicenna, of Augustine, Boethius, and others, but they can be summoned to appear together, confronted, and asked each one to say its last word, its ultimate truth. The theologian will then find himself in a position to take them all together to the higher truth of theology in which they can all unite because it lies beyond them all.

Pierre Duhem would have been right if the doctrine of Saint Thomas had been in his own mind the outcome of this incongruous mixture of various philosophies. But to credit Aquinas with such an intention is a mistake in history. The meaning of these philosophies in his mind follows from the theological criticism to which he submits them. Plato alone would never take the mind beyond the Idea of the Good; once there, the intellect could not proceed further along the same line. In the metaphysics of Aristotle, there is nothing beyond the Prime Immovable Mover. In the philosophy of Avicenna, after reaching the First, there still is no beyond. When it has arrived at the term of his own "way," each one of these philosophers naturally thinks he has arrived at the ultimate truth. None of them seems to have felt the slightest desire to come to terms with the others—far from it. A prisoner of his own "way," each one of them ignored the others. The only one who thought of a beyond in which they could unite was the theologian.

The unknown point of convergence to which he takes the philosophies of his choice is not for them simply a possibility; in the sight of the theologian who reveals it, it is for them the fulfillment of an unconscious desire. The theologian knows that the God to Whom each one of these philosophies tends and cannot reach is the only true God in Whom his own theology finds its starting point. Each philosophy follows only one way, but the theology of Saint Thomas sees five of them as so many stages on the ascent leading to I AM, the summit from which he himself watches and judges their progress toward Him. From the height of his faith, the theologian comes down to the philosophers, meets them on the road, goes along with them for a while, then, leaving them behind, hastens to their common goal and invites them all to join him. How can one charge with timidity and eclecticism a theology from which reason receives only invitations to intrepidity? *Quantum potes, tantum aude!* Happy the pagan philosophies that a tutelary theology thus takes beyond the term of their own itinerary! Such achievements have always been scarce in the past. From the time the true notion of theology was lost, they became practically impossible. No wonder, then, that our age has nothing but a failure to report in its own record. Still, this was such a noble failure that it deserves careful consideration.

THE
BERGSON
AFFAIR

When I consider that it took me about forty years to see what I had under my eyes and to learn what I could have read from the very beginning, I find it hard to believe. But this is what really happened to me. Only a change deep enough to obscure the nature of Thomistic theology, taking place between the thirteenth century and our own times, could explain the possibility of such a mistake. The immutability in which the schools sometimes take pride is often enough no more than apparent. For indeed they do change. It even happens that if, after a long period of time, they are confronted with the face of their youth, they do not recognize it as their own. Between 1905 and 1939, through uncertainties and at the price of many false starts, a Catholic philosopher was bound to waste much time in rediscovering notions that he should always have possessed.

I could have put these years to better use than in rediscovering my own past. Never was a present more deserving of attention than the one in which it was my privilege to live, in France, during the first third of the twentieth century. In philosophy, these years were for us the age of Bergson. For the first time since Descartes and Malebranche, France then had the good fortune to possess that rare being, a great metaphysician. I mean a man who, looking at the world and saying what he sees, leaves in the minds of men a renovated image; not indeed as the scientist, by discovering new laws or new structures in matter, but rather by penetrating further into the core of being. Bergson did just that. He did it under our very eyes, in our presence, in such a simple way that we were surprised not to be able to do it ourselves, introducing us to a new world as he himself was discovering it step by step. No words will adequately express the admiration, the gratitude, the affection we felt and still feel in our hearts for him.

To form a just idea of what this philosophy meant to us, one date should be kept in mind. Bergson was and remains before anything else in my memory the man whose first philosophical career ended, so to speak, with *Creative Evolution*. Whatever he published between the *Essay on the Immediate Data of Consciousness* and *Creative Evolution* came as from one single vein. Read, reread, and meditated ceaselessly, these works brought us an interpretation, complete in its principles though certainly not in its details, of the world and of man through whom the world arrives at self-awareness. We had the feeling of being formed by him and, as it were, introduced to a vision in which the universe was exposed in its intelligibility. In one sense, some of us never went beyond this point. Speaking for myself, I can say that the Bergsonian revelation ended in 1907, the year when *Creative Evolution* was published. By that time Bergson had given me all the help I could expect from him and he had said all that was profitable to me in his message. After that date, I continued to meditate his great books, but with the feeling that no new revelation was to be expected from him. However precious it could be, what he still might say would expand his message without enriching it. During the long interval of twenty-five years that separates *Creative Evolution* from *The Two Sources of Morality and Religion,* we knew that he was applying his genius to these problems, but we were awaiting the fruits of his meditations without any impatience. In fact, we were expecting nothing from him. His philosophy of nature had been for us a liberation. In this respect, I had contracted toward him a debt that nothing will ever make me deny; but the situation was different as far as religion was concerned. I had one, I knew what it was, and my very effort to deepen my knowledge of its nature turned me away from attempting other approaches. While I was thus living my religion, Bergson was still looking for one. How could I hope to receive enlightenment from him on an order of facts whose meaning he could not penetrate for lack of personal experience?

The Two Sources was published in 1932. Something unexpected then happened to me and I cannot explain it clearly. Still less can I justify it, for I am aware that there was an element of irrationality, not to say unreasonableness, in my reaction. After sending the author the usual compliments, I had the book carefully bound and placed it on a shelf in my library where it was to remain unread for years whose number I would be ashamed to acknowledge. Only the violence of my admiration for Bergson can account for such an attitude. I never confused philosophy with religion. If religion is truly at stake, then our whole life is involved. Now I knew that Bergson's book could not transcend the level of philosophy. This was a perfectly natural and reasonable fact; I would have accepted it from any philosopher whose thought had not become for so many years the food of my own. But that he, Bergson, could have embarked under my very eyes on a venture that was bound to fail, this was too much for me. Besides, the thing was done. It was no longer in my power to prevent the disaster, but I did not want to witness it.

I am not pretending that my attitude was reasonable; I am simply relating what I did. I felt reluctant to accompany a beloved master on a pilgrimage to a spring whose water I had been drinking from early youth. One does not find the sources of religion at the term of any philosophy, but beyond it. If one wishes to speak of religion, one must start from it, which has no source, but is the source. There is no other way to reach it. What I still wanted to know about religion was not anything that Bergson could teach me. A sadness held me back on the threshold of this last masterpiece, and it was only much later, after I had learned to my own satisfaction the meaning of such words as "faith" and "theology," that I could open the book without misgivings. From the very first page the old charm worked again. I had to lay the book down for short intervals, and at times to interrupt my reading. I felt like a man who wanted to slow down the tempo of a piece of music in order to prevent it from passing away, unmindful that it was necessary for it to pass in order to be. Still, my worst fears proved more than justified. It was not this or that idea, this or that development, that was out of focus; the whole book was out of focus. The author had established himself outside the focus of his subject and had remained there.

There was another cause for emotion. Reading the masterpiece from the vantage point of faith and in the perspective of time, I thought that the experience of a whole life was at last finding its true meaning. This philosophy of Bergson, so powerless to account for the nature of religion, could have been for Christian philosophers the occasion of a thoroughgoing re-examination of their own philosophy, the prelude to a new era of doctrinal creativeness and enrichment.

The task to be undertaken was not to reform Thomism in the light of the new philosophy. The truth theology lives by is that of the Christian revelation which is immutable. The Church cannot change her theology every time it pleases some philosopher to propose a new view of the universe. On the contrary, what had to be done was to transform the new philosophy in the light of Thomism. The call was not for an anti-Thomistic revolution by means of the philosophy of Bergson, but rather a revolution within Bergsonism effected by the theology of Saint Thomas Aquinas. The undertaking had become a legitimate one from the moment Bergson himself openly crossed the border between the two territories and, leaving that of philosophy, entered the domain of religion. But there was no one to undertake the task, so that we shall never know exactly what the result would have been. In this case, however, it is not philosophy that failed theology; all the philosophical materials required for such an undertaking were there, collected, ordered, and made ready for use by the genius of Bergson. Only, when the time came to purify and to order them in the light of theology, we discovered that wisdom had forgotten her time-honored function of guiding star. More simply, perhaps, she was busy elsewhere. At any rate, she was not interested.

Without a philosophy, *scholastic* theology is impossible. Theologies of this sort are as many as the philosophies from which they borrow their techniques. Without Plotinus, no Augustinian theology; no Thomistic theology without Aristotle. In order to prepare them for service, theologians often have to reconstruct and to perfect the philosophies they put to use; the result of their effort is the emergence of an improved philosophy and sometimes a completely transformed one. But theology does not create these philosophies, it finds them in existence and improves upon them by making them serve higher ends.

This is easily understood. Philosophy belongs in the temporal order. Like science and art it is naturally "of this world." As such, it is foreign to religious faith and in practice ignores it. This is indeed what makes its collaboration so precious every time theology can obtain it. If we want to show that the agreement between religious faith and natural reason is spontaneous, the voice of reason needs sometimes to be heard alone. Without a nature, there can be no grace. Bergson was offering to theology this doubly extraordinary opportunity, a philosophy obviously free from all links with religion and one which nevertheless was such that a Christian theology could use it to its own ends. Everything was ready for an operation that never took place. The theologians left it to the philosophers, who were not qualified to undertake it; they themselves were satisfied to criticize the results and to record the failures.

To an outside observer, who is not in the best position to judge, it would seem that the religious education of Bergson was not carried very far. His brethren in the same faith at times bitterly reproached him with insufficiently knowing his own religion. Let it be admitted that his religious instruction was superficial and of short duration. One must be very sure of oneself to assess the influence of a particular teaching on the mind of a youth, not only subjected to many other influences but also of such exceptional ability. I do not think that this influence was nil, but it must be conceded that, by and large, Bergson was a pure product of the French university education to which he was submitted during the decisive years of his intellectual training. This is particularly true of his years at the Ecole Normale Supérieure in Paris. No other school that I know could have produced such a typical example of "general culture," by which I mean a man equally able to publish a school anthology of Lucretius, to learn alone what he needed to know of the science of his own day, and to give to his contemporaries a philosophy of world-wide importance and to France the model of an unsurpassed philosophical style. Today young scribblers like to say that Bergson was a poor writer. They do not seem to know that the perfection of philosophical style is exactly to fit thought, and that only a philosopher is a good judge in the matter. However this may be, Bergson was imbued with the respect for scientific learning that was so widespread and deeply rooted in French minds in the second half of the nineteenth century. His adversaries were to remain Spencer and Taine, but he had to free himself from their influence before opposing it. Though opposed to scientism, Bergson was to keep all his life the love of knowledge based upon observable facts, and at least prolonging the line of experience when it cannot be experimentally verified.

This is so true of him that the scholastics have reproached Bergson with an excessive shyness in matters of metaphysics. I think they were right, and we shall have many occasions to verify their opinion. My present point is that the reproach should not have been leveled at him in the name of Aristotle; for though Aristotle was much more gifted than Bergson for metaphysical speculation, yet no philosopher resembles Aristotle more than Bergson in his love of empirical knowledge, his constant care to get hold of reality such as science knows it and to judge his conclusions in the light of experience. Scholastics have a remarkable way of forgetting that the proof of the existence of a Prime Immovable Mover first appears in Aristotle as the conclusion of his *Physics*. The Prime Mover of Aristotle was the summit of a cosmography of the fourth century before Christ just as the *élan vital* crowned in Bergson a cosmogony of the twentieth century after Jesus Christ. Different as they may be in many respects, Aristotle and Bergson never change their methods. When the time came for Bergson to enter the philosophy of religion, he began by asking himself: What does experience say about it?

To those who were, or thought they were, Aristotelians, the new philosophy offered in this respect unlimited possibilities of collaboration.

No, we were then told, Bergson has disqualified intelligence, and Aristotle was nothing if not an intellectualist. The attitude of Bergson toward intelligence was a very complex business. His philosophical speculation was imbued with such a respect for the methods of science that one suspects some misunderstanding behind the reproach. What did happen seems to be this. In a century when the true notion of intelligence had been lost, Bergson, starting from what was then the accepted notion of intelligence, undertook the task of submitting it to a much-needed critique. We shall have to return to this capital point. For the present, let us note that, far from despising intelligence functioning within the limits of the competence it then claimed, the philosopher of Bergson's persuasion was not supposed to remain content with the rational knowledge of things such as they were; he still had to do his utmost to make this knowledge fit more closely the manifold aspects of reality.

In this sense, the philosophy of Bergson constitutes a critique of a certain wrong use of intelligence conducted by a mind fond of accuracy and never satisfied with itself. True, Bergson did not trust intelligence to reach what is deepest in reality, but this was something the kind of intelligence he opposed was in fact unable to do. He opposed the bad use men make of intelligence when, pretending to speak in the name of science, they take advantage of this pretension to deny the possibility of metaphysics. There must be something wrong with a notion of intelligence that makes it unfit for metaphysical knowledge. Bergson wanted to revive metaphysics as a science, and since intelligence had disqualified itself to this end, it was necessary for the metaphysician to look elsewhere. In the order of science proper, Bergson simply reproached intelligence with its inaptitude to know those objects whose existence it denied precisely because it failed to grasp them.

In fact, Bergson always conceived philosophical research after the pattern of scientific research. One day he was entrusted by his colleagues with the thankless task of saying what the Collège de France had contributed to philosophy since the time of its foundation in the sixteenth century. This was not easy to do since, to be quite truthful about it, the only outstanding service the Collège ever rendered philosophy had been to appoint Bergson. Bergson himself could not very well say that. Still he did not shy away from the task. Not without some secret amusement he availed himself of the occasion to say "What Philosophy Owes to Claude Bernard." Now what philosophy owes to this biologist, according to Bergson, is a conception of scientific research such as philosophers would be well-advised to follow. "Philosophy should not be systematic," Claude Bernard had said. Echoing this startling statement, Bergson added that since our intelligence, which is a part of nature, is not as wide as nature, "it is doubtful that any of our present ideas are vast enough to embrace it." Then he added: "Let us work then to dilate our thinking, let us force our understanding, if necessary let us break our routines; but let us not narrow down reality to the measure of our ideas since it is up to our ideas to model themselves, enlarged, upon reality." This war waged against intellectual sloth does not indicate an enemy of intelligence. None understood this better than Charles Péguy, who was always in deep harmony with the spirit of the doctrine. He has said in one sentence all there was to say on this point: "Bergsonism does not consist in forbidding to oneself the operations of thought. It invariably consists in modeling these operations on the reality in question."

We thus find ourselves confronted by a philosopher perfectly suited for a theological experiment. The man is not a Christian; we are even told that he is not a good Jew; he thus exhibits the kind of paganism that recommends Aristotle to the scholastics of all times. Like that of Aristotle, the philosophical reason of Bergson approves of conclusions that are dear to Christian theology. One can thus be sure that, with Bergson, it is not a question of any religious apologetics; rather, we would be witnessing a truly remarkable phenomenon: a genuinely spontaneous accord between the Christian faith and the natural reason. Now it happened that, by a parallel good fortune, starting from the science of his day as Aristotle had done in his own, this new philosopher had early denounced as so many errors the scientism, materialism, and determinism that for their part the theologians considered their most dangerous enemies. Most important of all, Bergson was not satisfied with directing against these errors refutations invented by Aristotle against the scientism of the fourth century before Christ; he drew his criticism from the very science of the twentieth century whose conclusion they were intended to be.

For us, young Catholics in love with philosophy, this was a decisive event. Until then everything we had said in metaphysics was disqualified by objections that as Christians we could choose to ignore but that as philosophers we had no right to neglect. What about Kant and Comte? we were sometimes asked. We had no answer. All the excellent Reinstadler had to say on these points carried no weight: *Criticismus refutatur,*

positivismus refutatur. Coming from men who professed
a priori to reject as false all doctrines at variance with
Christian theology, these conclusions were certainly
right, but unfortunately they did not tell us why the
others were philosophically false. The arrival of Bergson on the battlefield changed the conditions and the
meaning of the fight. From that moment on the negation of metaphysics in the name of modern science
found itself counterattacked by the contrary affirma-
tions of a metaphysics inspired of this very science. Scientism now found itself on the defensive. Positivism
was routed by a philosophical spirit more positive than
its own. By showing himself more exacting in matters
of science than they had been, Bergson triumphantly
broke through both criticism and scientism.

One must have lived through these years to realize
what a liberation the teaching of Bergson was. At first
he himself was not clearly aware of the revolutionary
import of his teaching. Léon Brunschvicg asked him
one day how he himself felt about his thesis, "The Immediate Data of Consciousness," when he took the
manuscript to Jules Lachelier. "You must have known
it was something out of the ordinary," Brunschvicg said.
"Not at all," Bergson answered. Then, after a moment
he added: "On the contrary, I even remember I was
saying to myself: It is silly."

Bergson had had time to get used to his own ideas
when, in 1905, I read the book for the first time.
Nothing will ever revive for me the sheer delight of
this first contact. I would read and read again the first
chapter, so clear was it that, in it, Bergson had carried
the day. How can one describe briefly the nature of the
event? The conclusions were less important to us than
the way he reached them. Take Bergson's new approach
to the problem of quality, for example. What did our

neoscholastics say on this point? Strictly speaking, "quality is an accident that perfects a substance both in its being and in its operations." Though this was not to say something false, it was to say nothing useful. On the contrary, Bergson was calling attention to the experience of quality from the inside. Instead of describing it from the outside, he progressively brought his reader to perceive it such as it was in itself. In short, Bergson was teaching us to purify the category of quality from all contamination by that of quantity.

This first chapter of *The Immediate Data of Consciousness* was to have far-reaching consequences. By bringing his first effort to bear upon the notion of quality, Bergson had shown great metaphysical acumen. By so doing he was loosening the first mesh of the net woven by the determinism of quantity. For the first time since Comte and Kant metaphysics had waged war against scientific determinism on its own ground and won it. Through this break, all the rest was to follow. Psychological determinism was eliminated from the mind; freedom was restored in its rights and this not simply in virtue of some abstract piece of reasoning, but rather as an observed and personally experienced fact. At the same time, the soul was itself again, free from matter; and mechanical determinism, the first article of the materialistic creed, was brought back within its own bounds in nature as it had been in the mind. The term of this development was to be the notion of a world conceived as the work of a creative evolution, an ever-flowing source of inventions, a pure duration which, as it progressed, shed matter as a by-product.

We had repeatedly been told that metaphysics was dead. Our professors agreed on this one and only point, that metaphysics had ceased to exist. Lévy-Bruhl liked to repeat, with Comte, that metaphysics did not need to be refuted; it was of itself falling into disuse. Now the very thing we had hoped to receive from the Sorbonne, and had been refused, the Collège de France was giving to us with liberality. The Collège de France, this sole and unique teaching institution which, in France, is a state institution and yet free, how grateful to it we should feel, we, the young friends of metaphysics whom Bergson had found wandering in the desert of scientism and led out of it!

When in 1907 we could at last read, as in a sort of intellectual trance, the view of the world depicted in *Creative Evolution,* we could not believe our eyes. Of course this was somewhat above our heads. The book was the fruit of the long labor of a great philosophic mind. The doctrine it contained was such that it was almost an insult to accept it at first sight, as if one were then qualified to test its foundations, to calculate the resistance of the material, and to assess without error the solidity of the building. It was necessary to pause, to ponder on the doctrine, to walk personally in the philosopher's footsteps, in short, to embark upon this philosophical venture on one's own. But the winds seemed to be favorable. By a piece of luck so extraordinary that it seemed almost providential, theology had just come upon a pagan philosophy—all the more philosophy as it was the more pagan—which offered theology a soil in which nature is in proximate potency to grace, the only source from which its perfection can come to it. What was needed was another Thomas Aquinas.

We are still waiting for him. One hopes never to see again another example of the wisdom of theology so little anxious to discharge the task it rightly claims for its own. To judge the philosophers in the light of revelation, to redress their errors, to make up for their shortcomings, is a magnificent task; to achieve it, however, one needs first to have a thorough understanding of their philosophies. This is not done without effort. The example of what Thomas Aquinas did with Aristotle shows that it requires work and time. But in this affair, in which no one refused his labor, it was time that failed.

The first responsible were the Christian philosophers. In this juncture they behaved in accordance with their own traditions. For though they always begin by declaring that they do not intend to meddle in theology, that theology is above them and beyond their competence, no sooner have they laid down the principles of their own philosophy than they plunge headlong into theology and undertake a philosophical exegesis of the word of God. So did Descartes when, after proclaiming the separation of theology and philosophy in the *Discourse on Method,* he undertook to show that one could very well speak of the mystery of transubstantiation in terms of his own notion of matter, of substance, and of accidents.

This was doubly wrong. First, such as it is constituted, theology is not the work of any man, but of the Church, and no one can without extreme temerity undertake to reform it. Theology includes, besides the word of God, articles of faith, and dogmas that explicate them, conciliar decisions and their interpretations by great theologians when these are approved by the Church. Not one of these propositions has escaped being read, reread, discussed, and submitted to the close scrutiny of the Fathers of the Church as well as many Councils. Let it be remembered that what is at stake is to define the faith of the Church, which is its very life. In so doing, the Church has no intention of canonizing any particular philosophy; she simply intends to define with rigorous precision the truth she teaches and by the same token to eliminate all contrary error.

This is not any philosopher's business. At the San Francisco Conference, the famous jurist J. Basdevant approached a modest technical adviser responsible for the literary correctness of the French text. He put into his hands the part of the treaty related to trusteeships, and said: "Do not change one word in it. All these decisions have already been put to use and some of them are today recognized in the jurisprudence of the International Court of Justice of the Hague. Don't touch it!" This was wise. It is also wise for a philosopher to refrain from any personal intervention in an order of judgments that the pope himself pronounces solely in the name of the universal Church and on the basis of her tradition.

The Christian philosophers who intervened in the modernist quarrel were thus doubly ill-inspired. They interfered in a theology that they had not even taken the trouble to learn, but, more seriously still, they entered the problem from the wrong end. It was the theologian Thomas Aquinas who has assumed the responsibility of using the philosophy of Aristotle to give theology the form of a science; this time, on the contrary, it was philosophers who were enlisting the aid of Bergsonism for a theological restoration equally foreign to the intentions of the philosopher and of the theologians. It will be said that Christians had to take into consideration the philosophical revolution then in progress, and this is right, but they should have done so as philosophers, without undertaking, in the name of Bergson, a theological reformation that they were not qualified to carry out. It is not what they did. Full of ill-directed good will, one of them undertook to explain to the theologians the meaning of the word "dogma," as though the Church had lived so long without knowing it and needed his intervention to learn it. Others set about explaining to theologians the true and properly religious meaning of the word "God" on the ground that, until they came along, God had been imagined as a sort of "thing." Everything, they proclaimed, had been "reified," including God. If only they had expressed themselves with enough precision for us to know exactly what they wanted us to think in these matters! But such was not the case. Conciliar definitions may not please everyone but at least everyone understands their meaning. The so-called Bergsonian theology of a self-making God Whose being is an eternal becoming offered to the mind no definite meaning. It was not really equipped to handle this problem. Nor could the Church tolerate a disorder that she rightly saw as a pure and simple encroachment upon her authority and functions.

The temerity of these philosophers was felt by the theologians as a provocation, which in fact it was, but they too were under a delusion which, though contrary to the preceding one, was not without its own dangers. One can easily imagine Saint Thomas' attitude in such a situation. Or rather, we need not imagine it, we know it. Like the Saint Thomas of the thirteenth century, the twentieth-century Saint Thomas would have said: "Still another philosophy! What is it worth? Let us eliminate what is false in it; let us see what is true and lead it to its own perfection." Because Saint Thomas was a true theologian, the coming of a new philosophy was not a cause of panic for him. He knew how to handle it, which cannot be said for his modern successors, too many of whom had become philosophers. Each of them had his own separate philosophy, exclusively consisting of truths known solely in the natural light of reason. They had their own philosophical axe to grind and this was the main cause of the difficulty. Their dialogue with Bergson was supposed to be conducted between philosophers, and the only difference between them was that they happened to be Christians, often priests and theologians, whereas he himself was a religious agnostic. The philosophy they asked him to accept was not even the true philosophy found in the writings of Saint Thomas. Most of the time, it was some substitute, such as that of Cajetan or of Suarez. At any rate, they met Bergson on purely philosophical grounds, with the consequence that, in order to convince him, they should have been better philosophers than he was. Had they met him as theologians and relied on the light of theological wisdom, they could have done with him what Thomas Aquinas had once done with Plato, Aristotle, Avicenna, Averroes, and many other ones; that is to say, they could have shown him where his philosophy fell short of the truth and, at the same time, pointed out the higher source of light from which they themselves derived their certitude. Instead of one more dispute between philosophers, one would then have witnessed theology at work in the fulfillment of her perennial task.

The disorder was then at its peak. The theologians were behaving toward Bergson as philosophers, while their philosophy could not but be a philosophy of theologians. Now Bergson was neither a theologian nor a Christian. To judge him in the name of Christian philosophy was to impose on him duties that were not his; it was to exact from this philosophic intelligence, possibly the purest that the world had known since Plotinus, tasks that as a pagan he was not able to discharge. This was not all. By severing the philosophy of Saint Thomas from its theological sources, they divided the doctrine of the Common Doctor of the Church into two stumps, a separate theology on the one side and a separate philosophy on the other, and they allowed the ancient tree of Christian philosophy to wither on the ground. They had cut off its roots and dried out its sap. Whereas they had the opportunity to save a philosophy, thereby enriching themselves with new gold from Egypt, the Christian opponents of Bergson thought of nothing better than to exchange his philosophy for their own.

Such an offer had no chance of being accepted. Those who made it were all professing some form of neo-scholasticism. We know what kind of a philosophy this is. Whether it be an Aristotelico-Thomism, an Aristotelico-Scotism, an Aristotelico-Suarezianism, or any other member of the same family, it proposes to set up a body of philosophical doctrines such that, when the student comes to pass from the study of philosophy to the study of theology, he will not be held back by any fundamental divergence but rather will have only to complete his philosophy by theological conclusions. Such an undertaking is always successful because what is first constituted as a philosophy in it is, in reality, but a part detached from some theology in which everything has been done in the light of faith. When the time comes for theology to make use of such a philosophy, it merely recovers its own creation. If, on the contrary, one wishes to use it as a conventional philosophy in opposition to other philosophies likewise foreign to the Christian revelation, one must be ready for insuperable difficulties. The odds are on the philosopher. For though a Christian has the advantage as long as he philosophizes in the light of faith, he loses it as soon as he contents himself with philosophizing as though he were not a Christian.

Two facts were dominant in the situation. Christian thought had already gone through such a crisis in the thirteenth century, and, thanks mainly but not entirely to Saint Thomas Aquinas, it came out victorious. The oncoming Aristotelian tide then threatened to replace the truth of the Christian religion with some type of Aristotelian system that left to religion nothing more than faith and aimed to reserve for itself the exclusive use and benefits of reason. A deadly peril, which theology averted by demonstrating, first, that the sound philosophic use of reason in no way contradicted faith, and then that, on the contrary, a theology that was both prudent and bold could use the resources of philosophy to acquire within itself the form of a science. The enterprise was a success. This was chiefly because the philosophy of Aristotle is able to formulate in precise terms the most immediately evident data of sense experience. Aristotle himself had never aimed at anything else. His metaphysics often proceeds after the fashion of a dictionary. Whether the problem at stake is that of substance and accident, form and matter, act and potency, motion and rest, the philosopher merely asks: What is the meaning of these words in philosophy? That is why Aristotle's answers to these questions remain universally valid. It is possible to expound practically any system of philosophy in the language of Aristotle. This has often been done in the course of centuries; it is still being done today.

A mere glance at everyday language is enough to confirm the remark. The *matter* of a statue or of a lecture or of a discussion, the weakness in the *form* of a judgment, the *actualities* of a given situation, the *possibilities* of a project, such notions as *substance, essence, place,* and the whole vocabulary of the categories are as many examples on the point. Basically, Aristotelianism is first and foremost a language. Some consider this a weakness, and yet this is what insures its astonishing perenniality. There was therefore no reason why theology should not have successfully extended the use of Aristotelianism to the definition of the truths of faith.

The scholastics of the thirteenth century did it and with such success that the doctrine of one of them, Saint Thomas Aquinas, gradually became and was finally chosen as the norm of the teaching of the Church. It is well known that Saint Thomas has been proclaimed patron of all the Catholic schools and that the obligation to follow his teaching, today included in the Canon Law, has literally the force of law.

These well-known facts are briefly recorded here only to explain the state of mind of a Catholic confronted with the liberties that some Christian philosophers take with the discipline of the Church—and not only philosophers, but theologians as well. Such liberties are hard to understand. The extraordinary decision of the Church to select a certain doctrine as the norm of her teaching certainly cannot be taken as the expression of a mere preference that each person is free to judge as he pleases. Crowning centuries of a theological experience during which Thomism had been continually submitted to the test of discussion and criticism, this unique privilege conferred upon the theology of Saint Thomas has no meaning whatever if it does not signify that the Church recognizes in it the authentic and true expression of the faith of which it is the guardian. The most extraordinary thing about it, if it is permissible to express a personal opinion on this point, is that the better one knows Saint Thomas, the more clearly one realizes that the choice was good. Once more the Church was right. This is what makes it hard to understand how, on their own authority and for whatever philosophical preferences, some Catholics allow themselves to throw into confusion a doctrine officially approved by the Church as her own.

A second fact was then dominating the situation. Aristotelian philosophy, that universal philosophical

coin, of which Bergson himself rightly said that it out-
lined a "natural metaphysics of the human understanding," carried with it a physics and a cosmology that
though admirable in their time, are now out of date. No
doubt the physics of Aristotle was full of notions that
would remain universally and perpetually valid. A philosophy of nature has been drawn from it, a sort of
intermediary wisdom and, so to speak, a halfway house
between science and metaphysics, but Aristotle himself
did not see any difference between them. What we call
philosophy of nature was to him physics itself, the science of a universe of concentric spheres, eternally existing and eternally moved by their desire for a first form
pure of all matter, the Prime Immovable Mover. This
is a universe in which, with the exception of the Prime
Mover, who forever enjoys himself in the eternity of a
blessed life, everything is ceaselessly in motion and yet
nothing new ever happens. The world of Aristotle has
an everlasting existence, the heavens have eternally
accomplished their revolutions and are still doing so;
and even in our sublunar world, in which individuals
are endlessly coming to be and passing away, the species
are immutable, having always been what they now are
and will ever be. Corrected on the more critical points
on which it directly opposed the teaching of the Church,
for instance on the necessary existence of an uncreated
universe, the scientific and philosophical view of the
world formulated by Aristotle has been perpetuated in
neoscholasticism; and, on the whole, it continued to be
the doctrine used against Bergson by his scholastic opponents when, at the maximum of its virulence, the
modernist movement was condemned in 1907.

A crisis of conscience then developed among many
young Catholic philosophers open to the influence of
Bergson. It was not the so-called Bergsonian theologies

that disturbed them. Vague and unsubstantial, these were too visibly the work of self-appointed theologians. As I said above, these young men were ignorant of what theology really was, especially that of Saint Thomas; but they felt that the new theologies of the "as if," which, incidentally, were hardly Bergsonian, expressed in a very imperfect way the substance of their faith. On this essential point, the scholastics of the year 1900 were certainly right, but at the level of philosophy, their criticism was ineffectual. At this precise level, neo-scholasticism had nothing useful to say, whereas Bergson was to be found at the most advanced point of progress. If it is said that our scholastics at least saved the truth of faith, the answer is obvious: it is scholasticism that lives by faith, not faith by scholasticism. Those who survived this crisis were men who simply continued to pray God, asking Him to show them the light that was hidden from them or, rather, to which they were blind.

There are times when the universe undergoes abrupt changes in the minds of men. The thirteenth century was one of them. Christians then experienced the sudden revelation of what had been the science and philosophy of Greece. The sixteenth century was another such time. Tycho Brahe *saw* with his own eyes a comet going through one of the supposedly solid celestial spheres, thus for the first time in history proving their non-existence and at the same time wrecking the cosmos of the Greeks. The nineteenth century saw still another one of these revolutions. As the outcome of long and patient observations and reflections, Charles Darwin established in his *Origin of Species* that living species have not always existed with exactly the same characteristics that they possess today. At that very moment the vegetable and the animal kingdoms, such as Aristotle had conceived them, joined his cosmography in the world of lost illusions. The world of modern science differs from that of the Greeks in this, that it has a history. This unexpected confluence of nature and history, two orders that in the past had always been separated, not to say opposed, will remain for those who will look back to it from the future the distinctive feature of the late-nineteenth-century view of the world. Since then we ourselves have seen scientific universes tumbling upon one another with increasing velocity. Those of us who were born in the world of Newton have passed from it into that of Einstein, and we might be at a loss to say in which universe we are living today. The philosophy of Bergson itself lost its breath trying to catch up with the world of Einstein. Whatever one may think of it, one can hardly deny that with its insistence on change, becoming, duration—in short, creative evolution—Bergson's philosophy truly was that of the science of our own time.

The obstinacy of many scholastics in maintaining in a state of philosophical privilege the Greek cosmos of Aristotle is all the more difficult to understand because the universe of science was never closer to that of Scripture than it is today. The Old Testament relates the origin of the world as a story, that is to say, a sequence of moments in the course of which the diverse elements of the physical world, the vegetable and animal species, then man himself, appeared successively on the stage of the world. Nothing resembles this universe of Scripture less than the eternal and uncreated cosmos of Aristotle, peopled with species immutably fixed under their present appearances, and completely alien to history both in its origin and its duration. Assuredly, Scripture can do without science. It is as independent of the universe of Einstein as of that of Aristotle, and religious dogmas lie so far beyond the reach of laboratory demonstration that scientific revolutions will leave the Church unconcerned. There was therefore no reason for the theologians to follow after Bergson. Only, it is paradoxical that scholastics persistently used Aristotle against him on the very points on which his personal notions about the world were closer to the teaching of Christian dogma than was that of the Greek philosopher.

One of the harmful effects of this attitude was to create the false impression of an absolute doctrinal divergence between the philosophical thought of Bergson and that of Saint Thomas. On this point we have a choice witness in the person of Charles Péguy. For the Catholic critics of Bergson were Thomists, or so considered themselves, and since Péguy knew nothing about Saint Thomas Aquinas he believed them implicitly. All the attacks launched against Bergson in the name of Thomism were inevitably understood by him as a struggle between Bergson and Saint Thomas Aquinas in which Bergson even appeared to be the aggressor. One wonders how he could have been, since his complete ignorance of Thomism protected him on this point. Péguy was in a turmoil over the situation. Entreating the Catholic adversaries of Bergson to weigh the consequences of their attitude, he then warned them as follows:

Whatever will be taken away from Bergson will redound to Spencer, and not to Saint Thomas. And once more Saint Thomas will have nothing, and he will have no one. He will be as he was and what he was twenty-five or thirty years ago, before the coming of Bergson: a great saint of the past, a great doctor of the past, a great theologian of the past. Respected, revered, venerated. Without any hold on the present, without access, without that bite which is such a peculiar phenomenon, without that grip which alone counts . . . (A great doctor, esteemed, celebrated, consecrated, denumbered, buried.)

Péguy was only too right, except on two points. The Thomism of his time had indeed no hold on his contemporaries, but it was not Saint Thomas' Thomism, it was the Thomism of the Thomists. It had so little power to hold that whenever any attempt was made to restore it to its original boldness, its recognized spokesmen cried to heaven against such a scandal. I know of no theology that is freer and bolder than that of Saint Thomas. But how it has been domesticated! His deepest intuitions are regularly kept in the background.

My second reservation would have surprised Péguy still more if he could have foreseen the immediate future. It was not at all necessary that whatever was taken away from Bergson should be gained once more by Spencer. In fact, all that which certain Thomists wanted to take away from Bergson was in the end destined to redound to Saint Thomas Aquinas.

WISDOM TAKES A HOLIDAY

In his *Note conjointe sur M. Descartes* Charles Péguy announced his intention to write one of his fortnightly *Cahiers* on M. Bergson and the Catholics. It is a great loss that this intention was not fulfilled. "It would be a very short fascicle," Péguy added. This is doubtful, but it is absolutely certain that, had Péguy written it, this issue of the *Cahiers* would have severely castigated those whom he called *"les scholastiques"* (with an *h* in French), or still more directly the Thomists, for the blindness of their attacks against Bergson and their unfairness toward him.

One should not be too surprised by these attacks. Coming from the Thomists, they were a sort of compliment. After reading Kant and Comte, or Spencer and Taine, a Catholic theologian cannot enter *Creative Evolution* without having the impression of breathing better intellectual air. He feels that he has come to a friendly country. A modern philosophy which, at one strike, does away with mechanism, associationism, determinism, and in a word, as Péguy said, atheism: what an ally against formidable adversaries in a thus far unsuccessful fight! But this is precisely what annoys the theologian. He wonders why this philosophy, so well embarked on the right course, does not follow it to the end. *Elle a trop de vertus pour n'être pas chrétienne:* it is too full of virtue not to be Christian! This was really what one tried to convey to Bergson by honoring him with the choice severities that the Church does not squander on those whose case is hopeless. From there to treating such a doctrine as a potentially Christian philosophy is but a short distance and the Catholic critics of Bergson often crossed it.

I cannot help but think that this was a mistake, but after all I do not know. The secret face of conscience is open to God alone. Among those who still remember

Henri Bergson with affection, even though they have known him only as a venerated and beloved master, some will remember with gratitude what they owe him even in terms of their religious life. What is it? Not at all to have been Christians, not even to have remained such, but rather, as philosophers, to have been able to preserve their religious faith without feeling ashamed of their philosophy. The presence of Bergson reassured us. By itself it constituted what one could call the "proof by Bergson." Thanks to him, metaphysics, once banned by Kant, was being reinstated in France, and this in a twofold way: first, in fact, for with him the philosophical reason was a witness in favor of "preambles to faith"; but also by right, because Bergsonism did not content itself with rejecting Kantian and positivist errors, it explained their existence. Christian students of Bergson owe him too much for their hope not to be without reserve. Still, truth must be scrupulously respected, all the more so as the truth at stake in the present case is important for a proper understanding of Bergson's philosophy. It is that he was *not* a Christian.

I do not wish to contradict anyone on this point. I am not questioning in the least the authenticity of the remarks attributed to him by some of his friends and I admit that their interpretation raises delicate problems. I would rather say that this is a still more delicate question than those who have relayed his words to us seem to realize. With friends, Bergson was dangerously courteous. It is to their honor that they were not always aware of it, but the situation had its danger. One often perceives in the words attributed to Bergson, and which he certainly has said, the desire and even (it is tempting to say) the consummate art to authorize an interlocutor to think that he is being told what he wants to hear, without advancing one inch beyond the limits of what one wants to say. We have on this point a witness of great perspicacity. Before reading the priceless conversations with Bergson relayed to us by some of his Christian friends, it would be well to meditate on the admirable pages of Charles Du Bos's *Journal* for February 27, 1922, in which, after a visit to the master whose thought had molded his own "in its depth," he expressed disappointment at his failure to go below the surface of the social ego that Bergson always interjected between his interlocutor and himself. He "says just what he should say," Du Bos remarks, and goes on to describe the "small magician, secret, elusive, who performs in your presence as if always eager to retire within himself." What guarantees the correctness of so many "conversations with" Bergson is that while reading them we often have the impression that he is winking at us over the bent shoulders of the conscientious scribe.

I know how uncertain such impressions are, but each of us can report only his own. Those who think that they were taken more deeply into his confidence may well be right, but they may also be deluding themselves somewhat. Extremely sensitive to criticism, Bergson was no less so to approval and sympathy. At the risk of adding my own interpretation, I shall venture to say this. To understand the complex attitude Bergson had toward his Catholic admirers and friends, one must remember that nothing prepared him for the welcome they gave him. For this university professor, who was born in another religion and who moreover practiced none, Catholicism was something entirely foreign. Without any religious ties, he had, however, a *naturally* religious soul as did Plato, Aristotle, and Plotinus before him. If one remembers his scrupulous respect for facts, the unexpected meeting with young Christians, students, colleagues, and often also priests, who assured him of their philosophical and *religious* gratitude, could not but raise in his mind a curious problem. After all, was he not unawares, if not a Catholic, at least much closer to Catholicism than he knew? It was not in his character simply to reject such suggestions, nor in his mentality to accept them without thinking over what made them possible. I could easily believe that our master accepted in his heart Catholicism to the same extent his Catholic friends accepted Bergsonism. This could have led him rather far, but on a road different from theirs.

In saying that Bergson was never a Christian, I wish to respect entirely whatever secret there was in his conscience and limit myself to his public declarations and acts. What is a Christian? The catechism of my childhood answered: "A Christian is one who, having been baptized, believes and professes the religion of Jesus Christ." It is simply a fact that Bergson was never baptized and never professed the religion of Jesus Christ in the sense in which this catechism understood it, that is, including the truths the Christian must believe, the duties he must fulfill, and the means God has established for our sanctification. There is no point is discussing the famous expression he used in his will in 1927: "I would have become a convert if . . ." and the following. No *if* is permissible. For a Christian at heart, there is no conceivable reason not to receive baptism immediately. The desire of baptism is not the baptism of desire. However noble the reason offered by Bergson to explain his attitude—"to remain with those who tomorrow will be persecuted"—has no religious value. That such a feeling could balance in his heart the idea of his possible conversion shows well enough that what was at stake was still but a velleity; it was not a question of that supremely free act, in the Bergsonian sense of the term, which also presupposes the Augustinian notion of *libertas* or the "power" to act. All the words of Bergson are precious to me, and especially those of 1927. I even believe that in revealing to him "the complete fulfillment of Judaism," Christianity brought Bergson back closer than he had ever been to the religion of his fathers. Still, what comes out most clearly from this solemn declaration, in which every word counts, is that Bergson *was not converted.*

One fact helps us to understand that some theologians did Bergson the honor of dealing with him as though he were a Christian: there were Christians among the Bergsonians, and over these at least the theologians had authority. One of the characteristic traits of these Bergsonians was precisely the unscrupulous freedom with which they extrapolated the conclusions of the doctrine. It was truly surprising to see them extend to other fields, without first proceeding to one of those inquiries that the philosopher wanted to carry out in an exacting way sometimes over many years, conclusions that he himself held as valid only within certain limits. If one wanted to criticize Bergsonism, as it was the right of all and the duty of some, that of Bergson himself was certainly the first deserving of attention. Such a procedure would have avoided a great deal of confusion and wasted time.

One of the most objectionable points of Bergson's doctrine was his criticism of intelligence, taking the word in the sense in which he himself used it. It is at least doubtful that the fundamental opposition introduced by the philosopher between intellection and intuition was philosophically justified. At any rate this was a problem to be discussed by philosophers, but the theologians were upset at the very thought that the aptitude of intelligence to seize reality without distorting it could be questioned. For, they said, there was no religious faith, no Church, without dogmas. Hence, if intelligence is unable to seize reality such as it is, then the very formulas of Christian truth will be out of its reach, and the knowledge of these truths will thereby become impossible.

All this was true, but it had no particular bearing on the philosophy of Bergson. As a first answer the philosopher could observe that the proposition: *intelligence should be able to grasp religious dogmas,* being essentially theological, did not concern him at all. It should have concerned a Christian, which he was not. The only problem he had raised was to know whether the intellect was equally fit to know all the different types of reality given in experience. Whatever the answer may be, the problem at stake is a philosophical one. Let them criticize his answer to this precise problem, if they choose; the rest is irrelevant.

Very well, the theologian will say, but since reason cannot contradict faith, your philosophy is bound to be erroneous if it cannot solve the problem. At least, your philosophy should not make the solution impossible. Let this be granted; then, to make sure that the doctrine of Bergson renders impossible the assent of the intellect to the formulas of religious dogma, one should first examine its meaning. Bergson has said that "intelligence is characterized by a natural incomprehension of life." Here, again, let it be clear that I am not at all convinced of the point, which is a debatable one, but Bergson has never said that this purely negative characteristic was the very essence of intelligence. If it does not understand life, intelligence does not consist in this lack of understanding. Moreover, it is not a priori evident that religious dogma presents itself to the mind with the attributes of mobility, change and the continuous invention of new forms which, in the doctrine of Bergson, characterize life; hence one cannot affirm a priori that a Bergsonian philosophy makes no provision for an intellectual object of knowledge such as religious dogma. For the sake of argument one would rather maintain that there are only two truly exact sciences, mathematics and theology, of which one is not knowledge because it is without an object, while the other is real knowledge because it has an object. In both cases the intellect proceeds by way of inference from propositions initially defined, and since, in the case of theology, these given propositions are also necessarily true (as warranted by the divine infallibility), one can add that it is the only science that is both necessary and real. This is not intended as a recommendation of the Bergsonian notion of intelligence. I wish only to suggest that, had he been consulted on the question and (this is rather doubtful) had he been willing to answer it, Bergson himself might have observed that, his critics to the contrary, intelligence such as he conceived it was characterized by an outstanding aptitude to lay down the stable and clear-cut formulas of dogmas united by strictly defined relations.

The theologian, especially if he speaks in his capacity as a judge, should not bother about these distinctions. Since he is a keeper of the faith, his point of view on these notions is necessarily different from that of the philosopher. What a writer intends to say, God alone knows with certainty. The judgment of a theological judge bears only upon what an author says taken according to the meaning of his words when these are used correctly. If the meaning they have for the author himself is erroneous, he is naturally responsible for his error. If his judge misinterprets the sense of a proposition, such a misunderstanding was possible, and though the fault lies with the interpreter, it is still the author of the proposition that is accountable for it. Meaning and misinterpretation are both his responsibility: meaning because it is erroneous, misunderstanding because the faulty language used by the author makes the misunderstanding possible. A proposition whose meaning does not appear clearly or is susceptible of an erroneous meaning is an uncertain proposition. In doubt, it is prudent to censure. In the case of a Catholic philosopher, censure is accepted beforehand, not only without protest, but with gratitude. And we must say why. It is that one can always be more precise, more accurate, more exacting toward truth than one ordinarily is toward one's own language. Censure is a somewhat unpleasant but wholesome admonition to think better or to write better. If, as in the case of Bergson, the writer is not a Catholic, the nature of the problem escapes him. The admonition may be useful for others; it is lost to him. It would even have been a loss of time to ask Bergson what he thought of it. This scrupulously honest mind would have no doubt answered: I think nothing of it; I never thought about the question!

The function of a judge is not the only one a theologian has to fulfill. It may not even be the most important one. One should sometimes try to figure out what Saint Thomas' criticism of the philosophy of Aristotle would have been if he had carried it out solely from the point of view of Catholic orthodoxy. The reading of the later writings of Saint Bonaventure can give us some idea of it. Instead of such a criticism, but without remaining silent before error where he sees it, Saint Thomas begins by undertaking a philosophical elucidation of the doctrine of the Philosopher. He is anxious to understand what Aristotle says in the very sense in which he says it, in order to profit from it if what the Philosopher says is true and, if the Philosopher is mistaken, to trace back his error to its source. When one has understood an error as error, one should be able to make a philosopher see it. Were the philosopher still with us, it ought to be possible, starting from his own position of a problem, to put him back on the way to truth. At any rate, this should enable us to safeguard his present-day disciples against the danger of straying with it. This supposes that the theologian is as able to philosophize as the philosopher. As a judge, the theologian can be satisfied to denounce from the outside what he considers to be false, but this does not affect the philosophical aspect of the problem. As wisdom, theology cannot rest with so little to say.

This is something that many of those who took Bergson to task for his own notion of intelligence failed to realize. They told him and told him again that his doctrine was erroneous on this point; they opposed their own doctrine to his, which of course was the thing to do, but no one whom I can remember took the trouble to re-examine in the light of his own principles the problem that Bergson had tried to solve. These Christian thinkers were delighted to see him fighting with them against the same foe, scientism; but in objecting to the Bergsonian notion of intelligence, they were taking away from their ally the very weapon that had insured his victory. Without Bergson, the scholastics could do little more than to persevere in their own doctrine. Speaking as judges, they simply said to Bergson: since our own notion of intelligence is true, and is different from yours, yours is false. Such a refusal of the Bergsonian notion of intelligence had for its result to leave untouched the difficulty Bergson had tried to remove. He himself had conceived this notion of intelligence as the only answer he could find to his problem. They were rejecting his solution but had none other to offer. The obstacle had not been cleared.

What was the obstacle? The very same one that since Kant and Comte, Spencer and Taine, had rendered the very possibility of metaphysical knowledge inconceivable, and that the Bergsonian notion of intelligence aimed to eliminate. Bergson's criticism certainly missed the true notion of intelligence, but it did hit the wrong notion of intelligence invented by the mechanical associationism of Spencer and Taine. Now this particular notion of intelligence was responsible for all the errors which, no less than Bergson himself, the scholastics were eager to destroy. The philosophy of Bergson had the immense merit of accounting for the very genesis of these errors. In order to obtain this result, the philosopher had had to carry the discussion on the ground occupied by his adversaries and to raise the problem in terms familiar to our own contemporaries: How is it that, by an almost irresistible natural tendency, intelligence has bent all its energies to one aim, to achieve a mechanistic and deterministic interpretation of reality?

This error is committed by many conservatives in more than one field. They imagine that things are self-conserving, so that to conserve them means doing nothing. Far from it. Theologians and philosophers teach on the contrary that things are conserved in the same way in which they are created. Truth is no exception to this rule, since, though it does not change after it has been found, everything around it changes, and if no effort is made to keep alive the feeling of its presence, it will soon be forgotten. It is still there, but it has become unrecognizable.

One of the chief functions of wisdom is precisely to maintain truth under the eyes of men. Where was it, then, and what was it doing at the time of the modernist crisis? It would seem that wisdom takes occasional holidays. At such times, apparently tired of having taught truth for so long, it seeks relaxation in compiling lists of errors. As has been said, this too is one of its functions, and by far the easiest one! We are indebted to it for the treatises *On the Errors of the Philosophers* so numerous in the thirteenth century. There were indeed many errors to condemn, but it was better by far to put truths in their place. This more difficult part of the task was fulfilled by Saint Thomas Aquinas.

The idea that guided him in his work seems to have been that, when a man teaches an error, one will free him from it not merely by telling him that he is wrong, but rather by expressing in a better way the very truth he was trying to formulate. It is like taking the wrong road. He who tells us that we are not on the right road certainly helps, but not as much as the man who gives us the proper directions to get there. Saint Thomas had done this for the Aristotelians, with the unavoidable consequence that he was accused of being one of them. But the future was to vindicate him. Who, in our day, has shown himself competent to do the same thing for the philosophy of Bergson? I see no one. Instead of submitting his doctrine to a reinterpretation in the light of faith and of theology, our Christian thinkers rather judged it from outside and denounced its shortcomings. The problem was not to turn Bergsonism into a Christian philosophy, which it was not and could not be since its author was not a Christian. The task to be performed was for Christian philosophy to reveal to Bergsonism, beyond its own limits, the deeper truth of which it was the bearer without being aware of it. No Thomist that

I can remember was available to reconsider the whole problem as only a theologian was qualified to do. The new Aristotle has not found his Thomas Aquinas.

The nature of the problem is better seen within the perspective of natural theology. We all remember the objections raised by theologians against the conclusions of *Creative Evolution.* The Bergson Congress of 1959 in Paris was for them an occasion to show that they were still of the same mind. The God of Bergson, they said, was a God immanent in the universe, of which in a way he was the cause, but of which in another way he was a part. Moreover, in keeping with the deeper inspiration of the doctrine, this Bergsonian God was not being but becoming. Ceaselessly creating himself, so to speak, the Bergsonian God is continually acquiring that which he still lacks to increase his perfection. Hence it follows that the God of Bergson is neither immutable nor perfect nor actually infinite; in short, he is not the Christian God defined by the Councils as infinite in perfection, eternal and immutable. One must choose between the God of *Creative Evolution* and the "immutable spiritual substance" of the Vatican Council.

Bergson had some reason to be surprised. His own effort had aimed at achieving a philosophical interpretation of the world of science and, more precisely, at showing that facts were inconsistent with a mechanist interpretation of biological evolution. It is only a theologian in haste who, himself in possession of a truth come to him from another source, substitutes God every time Bergson writes "vital impulse" or "creative evolution." This is to approach the problem from the wrong end, for if only philosophy is involved, no notion of God can be presupposed as true and forced on the philosopher. It is the theologian who proceeds from God to creatures, thus imitating the knowledge that God has

144

of creatures by knowing Himself. On the contrary, the philosopher proceeds to God from things and, in his capacity as a philosopher, he feels authorized to say nothing of the invisible First Principle save what can be known in this manner. We rightly say "nothing," a word which goes unheeded, and yet one which should be respected to the letter. Bergson did respect it. He scrupulously followed this properly philosophical way, and he did so without any merit on his part since he knew no other one. Not having to protect his mind against the influence of any religious faith, he did his work as a philosopher no less calmly than Aristotle had done, in the same ignorance of the decisions of the Lateran and Vatican Councils. It is true that, in *Creative Evolution,* his philosophy falls short of the God of Christian philosophy, but the same is true of the god of Aristotle. To imagine the contrary is to yield to an illusion which, widespread as it is, nevertheless is an illusion.

Creative Evolution is essentially a philosophy, and even, in the Aristotelian sense of the word, a physics. It is in his own *Physics* that, after studying motion, Aristotle finally came to posit the existence of a Prime Immovable Mover. Distinct from matter and, as such, *super*-natural, the god of Aristotle nevertheless remains a highest among other gods, the first of the separated substances from which, through the movement of the celestial spheres, come the generations and corruptions in our sublunar world. Keystone of the cosmos, the Prime Immovable Mover is included within it. He is separated from matter, not from the world. When Aristotle transfers him from his physics to his metaphysics this god retains the same nature. First among the gods, he remains the cause of causes, the first of a series of which it is itself a part, as inseparable from its universe

145

as the vital impulse of Bergson is from the world it creates. Since Christian theology had been able to make good use of the god of Aristotle so wholly foreign to all notion of creation, it must have become pretty helpless not to know what to do with the creationist philosophy of Bergson.

The theologian will say that the two cases are not comparable. What makes it impossible to accept the god of Bergson is not so much his immanence in the world; it rather is that, like the world itself, he is forever becoming. The beauty of the god of Aristotle is, on the contrary, that it is *immobile*. This is what makes him so capable of being assimilated by Christian theology. Being an immovable substance, he can be conceived as perfect, eternal, immaterial, and therefore infinite. In short, the god of Aristotle is not incompatible with the immutable and spiritual substance set forth by the Vatican Council. Bergson himself was to recognize the fact in his later work, *The Two Sources of Morality and Religion:* the reflection of Aristotle finally led him to the notion of a static god, and this god "was adopted with some modifications by most of his successors."

All this is true, but it is true only of the god of Aristotle and provided one does not include among the successors of the Philosopher, as has recently been done by a theologian, "the great Scholastics and the whole body of the Christian philosophers." The god of Aristotle could not have been included in the main stream of Christian thought unless he had first lost his Aristotelian characteristics and become the God of Scripture. Such a metamorphosis goes far beyond what are usually referred to as "some modifications."

To make a long story short I shall note only one of these "modifications," but it is one whose consequences are endless. The god of Aristotle is indeed immovable, but through no merit of his; it is easy enough for him to be immovable since he does nothing; he is a sluggard god. A self-thinking thought and thereby an eternally blessed life, he is not even the efficient cause of movement in the world, as a man is the cause of the movement of a stone by pushing it; he moves the universe only inasmuch as he is desired by it. He is a god who lets himself be loved, without knowing it or even caring about it. It is rather easy to conceive as immobile this god who is wholly wrapped up in himself and unconcerned with a universe he has not created. On the contrary, the God of Christian theology, the God it reaches when, engaging the services of philosophy, it tries to conceive Him as the cause of His creatures, this God is essentially a Creator. Unlike that of Bergson, the Christian God is not in the making, but, unlike that of Aristotle, He makes. It even is because He has made something that we know He exists. We know him, Saint Paul says, *from the things that are made.*

The God of Christian theology, then, cannot be accurately described in terms of any particular philosophy. Like the god of Aristotle, He is immobile, but like the god of Bergson He is creative. In other words, the Christian God is not immobile as a being, an act that does not act, nor is He becoming as a god who creates but who, in creating, creates himself and changes. The God of the Christian religion transcends all the gods of philosophy. What then did Saint Thomas do? He did this extraordinary thing. He proposed a new notion of God, accessible to natural reason as much as such a highly metaphysical notion can be, but one from which the notion of an immobile God and that of a creative God were both equally possible. In a way Saint Thomas owed this notion to Scripture, particularly to the passage of Exodus in which God Himself said that His name was HE WHO IS; but he also owed it to the natural reason and to philosophy, for this was a new way to conceive being.

In the theology of Aristotle, God had been the pure act of self-thinking thought; in the theology of Saint Thomas, God was likewise a pure act, hence immobile, but a pure act of being, hence a possible cause of existence for other beings. Saint Thomas says so in terse words: "Everything acts inasmuch as it is in act. Now to act is to communicate oneself forasmuch as one is in act; and since the divine nature is supremely act, it communicates itself supremely in all possible ways. One of these ways is to beget a being of the same nature, which is what happens in the generation of the Word; the other is to create, that is to say, oneself a being to cause others to be." Hence there is no question of unsaying that God is an immobile spiritual substance; it is simply a question of saying the whole truth. This Saint Thomas does by stipulating that this substance is the pure act of being, thereby transforming the whole meaning of the question. For if God is a pure act of being, it becomes possible to conceive God as immobile and, at the same time, as begetting, proceeding, creating. This is to leave the pagan world of Aristotle and to enter the Christian world of Saint Thomas Aquinas.

One can therefore understand that, anxious as they were to safeguard the truth of faith, as it was their duty to do, theologians felt bound to reject the "vital impulse" of Bergson as something that was not, but merely became. They were right in doing so, but they did it in a way that was unprofitable to themselves as well as to Bergson. I do not know what Bergson would have said if his critics had been Thomists instead of being Suarezians. No one can guess how he would have reacted to the notion of being conceived as that which is in virtue of an act of its own. The fact is that Bergson never heard of it. Still, there is no reason to think that he would not have understood the meaning of the notion. He then would have been offered a way to overcome his own notion of creative evolution and of the vital impulse. He could have included these notions under the all-embracing notion of being conceived as the immobile-in-itself, yet able to act because it is itself act. Unfortunately, they were ceaselessly repeating to Bergson that the God of Christian theology was that of Aristotle who not only did not create himself but created nothing. Bergson can be excused for having understood nothing of what he was being told. His Christian interlocutors were not wanting in intelligence or in charity. If they told him nothing of the Thomistic notion of God, the only notion that could take him beyond his own error to the truth they were trying to express, the reason is that they themselves had forgotten it.

In order to give a concrete meaning to what I wish to say, I beg to quote the name of a man whom, despite my remarks, I hold in reverence.

If there ever was a theologian anxious to understand Bergson, an intellect able to understand him and a priestly heart burning with the desire to win him to the Christian faith, it was A.-D. Sertillanges, O.P. He went so far in his effort to do justice to what was true in the philosophy of Bergson that his superiors put him under obedience to write another book to warn students against the errors to which his teaching exposed them. Sertillanges did so in the booklet he published in 1943 under the title *Lumières et périls du bergsonisme*. Reproaching Bergson with having misinterpreted the true meaning of our doctrines, particularly in that he conceived the Christian God as an inert being, this theologian energetically objected: "How could *we,* instructed as we are in the trinitarian processions, turn the divine immutability into a death?"

Nothing is more pertinent. For, unless one speaks senselessly, a pro-cession is something that proceeds; it goes forward, it marches on, it even goes out: *procedit in aciem, procedit ex portu.* It is true, Saint Thomas says, that it is here a question of an internal procession, somewhat in the way in which a thought proceeds from the mind without going out of it. To think is not to move, yet it is to act. At any rate, we are here involved in the mystery of faith: *et sic fides catholica ponit processionem in divinis.* Bergson could understand all this, even though he could not believe it. But when one tried, as did Father Sertillanges, to make him admit that this "proceeding" God was also and at the same time the "being *qua* being" of Aristotle, Bergson found himself confronted with an insuperable difficulty. Why should the "being *qua* being" of Aristotle proceed? How could he create? He does not do so in the philosophy of Aristotle, but God does both in the doctrine of Saint Thomas Aquinas, and He is eminently qualified to do so, because He is HE WHO IS, the pure act of existing.

This is what a Thomist should have said, but many Thomists of that time were in reality Suarezians. Such as they conceived Him after the manner of Aristotle, God had not the dynamic immutability of an act of being; rather He had the static immutability of an essence whose perfection consisted only in being perfectly what it was and in so remaining eternally. To those who were satisfied with such a theology the most innocent Bergsonian reference to any dynamism within the divinity sounded suspicious. In losing the God of Saint Thomas the Thomists had also lost his perfect freedom in the use of language when he did not wish any particle of truth to be lost. Now there is at least one sense in which mobility can be ascribed even to the Christian God. For it is true that God is unmoved, as is said in Malachias (3:6), "For I am the Lord, and I change not." But Scripture also speaks of God as being in motion, since it is written of wisdom (Wisd. 7:24) that she is "more active than all active things: and reacheth everywhere by reason of her purity."

There is no trace of Bergsonism in Saint Thomas. It would even seem that he wrote the fourth lecture of his commentary on the *Divine Names* to remove from our notion of God the last trace of change. God is unmoved in Himself. Still, it would have been opportune to remember that the problem posed by Bergson was to find a creative cause of universal becoming, of which it cannot be denied that it exists at least in the world. Now when it is a question of conceiving God as the creative cause of other beings, a thing which Aristotle never had to do, it is not enough simply to reaffirm His absolute and perfect immobility. Human language then finds at its disposal no other terminology than that of motion. This also is the language used by Dionysius, and which Thomas Aquinas does not condemn, but qualifies: "God is said to be moving inasmuch as He brings all things to existence and contains them all within His own being." Had Bergson been led to this notion of an entirely transcendent God, Whose nature no human language fits with perfect adequacy, neither that of immobility nor that of motion, he might perhaps have felt the necessity of positing above the *élan vital,* a first principle of the universe still caught in the flux of the becoming it causes, a God able to cause it without letting Himself be carried away by it. This would have been a God very close to that of Christianity, and very different from both the *élan vital*

151

of Bergson as well as the Unmoved Mover understood after the manner of Aristotle. From such a notion of God, however, what was true in the Bergsonian notion of evolution would have remained a possibility. Bergson himself would have heard it said that there was at least one Christian philosopher in whose doctrine a language similar to his own could lawfully be used, namely, Saint Thomas Aquinas. He would have learned from him that this unmoved God nevertheless moves and proceeds toward all creatures, since He is present by essence to all beings as well as to their operations. However, this truth was to be understood as theologians would understand it, in a way befitting God: *Quando sacrae scripturae doctores dicunt Deum, qui est immobilis, moveri et ad omnia procedere, intelligendum est sicut decet Deum.*

I have failed to find the slightest allusion to this aspect of the Christian truth of Saint Thomas Aquinas in the censures directed against Bergson. He deserved to be censured, but by Christians speaking otherwise than as Aristotelians. He would then have been profitably censured. But the reproaches directed against him left in obscurity the aspect of the doctrine that could have done justice to the intimations of truth contained in his philosophy. Saint Thomas too had known well that God was unmoved, but he had made no mistake about the nature of His immobility.

THE
UNINVITED
HANDMAID

There are times when a person must have the courage to provide the critics with an easy method to get rid of him. To say *I am a Thomist* is one of them. And it is practically infallible. He is a Thomist, they say: he himself says so; he is still living in the thirteenth century; there is no point in bothering about what he says. Another temptation to offer the critics is the one I am about to test. It consists in saying that if we Thomists have not helped Bergson to understand himself, on the contrary, he, Bergson, has helped us to understand Saint Thomas all the better. If perchance the critics happen to understand Saint Thomas otherwise than we do, they will account for the difference by saying that we have bergsonified Saint Thomas Aquinas.

Still it is better to say the truth even when it cannot be done without inviting misinterpretations. I shall therefore say what I believe I know from personal experience. I shall do it in the full awareness of the fallibility of my testimony and of my inability to demonstrate the truth of what I say. No one can know with certainty how the body of certitudes he calls his own thought progressively constituted itself. It is all the more difficult as its elements are not bound together by relations of efficient causality, but rather of harmony and purposiveness. I am not aware that a single Bergsonian thesis enters into my interpretation of Saint Thomas. On the contrary, I feel convinced of two things. Father Sertillanges has written: "Bergson has largely been wrong about our doctrines; let us not repay him by being wrong about his own." And he was right, with, however, this precision: that we ourselves were not entirely right about the meaning of our own principles. Father Sertillanges is an outstanding example of what I mean; at least he is if it is true, as I am afraid it is, that he never suspected the authentic meaning of the

Thomistic notion of *actus essendi:* the act in virtue of which an essence actually is, or exists. The only meaning he ever found in what he himself called "the famous distinction of essence and existence" was that "all things, save only God, need to be created." So what he missed in the metaphysics of Thomas Aquinas was precisely the notion of being that could have opened a new path to the metaphysical speculation of Bergson. The second thing of which I feel convinced is the truth of another remark of the same Father Sertillanges, which I take pleasure in approving unreservedly. Bergson, he also said, "can certainly help us to understand ourselves, by obliging us to stress aspects of our own positions which, without him, we would feel tempted to neglect."

This is exactly what did happen. In order to make clearer what I mean, I shall say that by breaking up habits of thought too favorable to the spirit of decadent scholasticism, Bergson created in us such a state of mind that, even without our having explicitly to ask the question, it was becoming impossible for us to believe that the commonly accepted interpretation of Saint Thomas was faithful to his thought. Our problem has not been to make Saint Thomas say any of the things that Bergson had taught us, but the Bergsonian fidelity to concrete reality opened our ears to words that Saint Thomas had kept repeating to us and which, nevertheless, we had failed to hear. No doubt, something within us had for a long time wanted to hear these words, or otherwise we too would once more have left them unheard. All real influences presuppose pre-existing affinities. This kind of service deserves to be acknowledged, as Father Sertillanges further said. I want to acknowledge it, not so much to ask indulgence for Bergson's errors, as to express my gratitude for the truths he taught us.

What I have just said can be clear only to those who

know something of the history of Christian philosophy
in our day. I do not intend to retrace it, and the reader
would soon feel discouraged. I wish only to give him
a reason to believe me when I advance the proposition
that I myself acknowledge as sounding quite unbelievable. At the beginning of the twentieth century, in
Western Europe, in the teaching of Catholic schools
and among scholastics who considered themselves
Thomists, the true meaning of the philosophy of Saint
Thomas had been lost. Unfortunately, I realize that the
reason is still less believable than the fact it explains.
The truth of the case is that, ever since the end of the
thirteenth century, which was the century of Saint
Thomas himself, this evil has been endemic to the teaching of Christian philosophy. This can be proved. Every
metaphysics rests on a certain way of understanding
the first principle, which is the notion of being. He who
understands it differently from Saint Thomas also understands Christian philosophy differently and thereby
professes another philosophy. In the sixteenth century,
the Dominican Dominic Bañes, one of the most competent commentators of the *Summa Theologiae*, after
recalling the fundamental truth that, in Saint Thomas,
the act of being (*esse*) was, within every being (*ens*),
the act of acts and the perfection of perfections, added
this impressive remark: "This is what Saint Thomas
ceaselessly inculcates and the Thomists refuse to hear."
Et Thomistae nolunt audire. I would content myself
with much less in describing the situation obtaining
at the beginning of the twentieth century. Let us say
that there still were so-called Thomists rejecting the
notion of being upheld by Saint Thomas Aquinas, and
it so happened that quite a few of them could be found
among the neoscholastic opponents of Bergson. Things
are slightly different today. What Bañes considered the

correct interpretation of the Thomistic notion of being has been spontaneously rediscovered by some of our own contemporaries, and it is worthy of note that among these there is hardly one who, at one time or another, has not been under the influence of Bergson.

Among the reasons for the sometimes peevish hostility displayed by certain scholastics against Bergson, some were justified. I shall quote some of them. I even feel afraid to appear harsher than I want to be. But all the reasons for their hostility were not equally pure. One would have showed more indulgence toward his criticism of intelligence if what he was attacking under this name had not so dangerously resembled the wrong use his critics themselves were making of it. There would have been enough to blame in his doctrine without looking for pretexts.

Another avoidable cause for misunderstanding was comparing the philosophy of Bergson with that of Saint Thomas as if they were philosophies of the same nature. That of Saint Thomas is nothing if it is not a Christian philosophy; that of Bergson could not claim to be one since he himself was not a Christian. The philosophies professed by neoscholastics who attend daily Mass and in some cases say it, are also Christian philosophies; only, prompted by the desire to look modern, it pleases them to deny the fact. Besides, most of them sincerely believe it. These Christians finally succeed in making themselves believe that their philosophy is essentially unrelated to their religion. In itself, the fact is without importance because no one believes them, but they feel thereby entitled to expect from non-Christian philosophers doctrines as perfectly attuned as theirs to the requirements of the Christian faith. This is not quite fair. It is even not too intelligent, but relations with others become complicated when we lose sight of the nature of what we are doing.

There was no justification for expecting from Bergson what cannot be expected from any pagan philosophy. He had never pretended to be anything else than a philosopher, and a philosopher practicing philosophy as the biologist Claude Bernard had understood science, taking only one step at a time, even if it cost him ten years of research work to take it. The scholastics who criticized him had themselves little experience of this way of philosophizing. Knowing their main conclusions in advance, they looked in the main for a philosophy that would support them. On the contrary, Bergson did not know ahead of time whither he was going; truly starting *a creatura mundi* as Aristotle had done before him, he courageously proceeded toward an unknown reality hidden behind experience and of which he could not guess what it would be. His Christian critics urged him to conclude as they themselves had already done. With a lack of intellectual tactfulness that was almost unbelievable, they already charged this scrupulous philosopher with errors they felt sure he was bound to commit, although they themselves were naturally unable to foresee the course the thought of Bergson would take, because philosophizing is a free act. Bergson himself could not have told them where he was going. How often did he not complain about this to his Catholic friends! They were pressing him to make premature doctrinal decisions for which, as a philosopher, he was not yet ready. His scruples in this regard were extreme. One cannot imagine a state of mind more different than his from that of the Christian friends who were trying to make him subscribe wholesale to a system of ready-made conclusions.

Bergson himself was fully aware of the situation. In Father Sertillanges' little book on their conversations, *With Henri Bergson,* a precious testimony that so greatly honors them both, he can be seen inviting the philosopher to the ultimate doctrinal decisions which, purely philosophical in appearance, would in fact have turned him into a Christian. This is what makes these conversations so interesting. A perfectly tactful man, Father Sertillanges would not have forgiven himself if he had bluntly told Bergson that he should become a Christian, but he felt no difficulty in urging him to philosophize as if he were a Christian, which in fact was the same thing. He could not see the point because, in his own mind, Father Sertillanges was not aware of philosophizing otherwise than as non-Christians around him were doing. Small wonder, then, that when Father Sertillanges went so far as to mention religious dogmas in his presence, Bergson would point out the reason he could not follow his interlocutor on this ground. Concerning the Incarnation, the philosopher saw and said that this was a religious belief situated exactly in prolongation of his own philosophy, only beyond it. He would then say: "I have no method to rise up to it." Again, speaking of the identity of the Church with Jesus Christ, Bergson once said: "There too I would not like to commit myself, for fear they would tell me: he always was a Catholic; his alleged method was but a round-about way for him to get where he wanted to be." In Bergson's own mind this was killing two birds with one stone. He was serving the truth of the Christian religion because, by refusing to make his philosophy say more than it had a right to do, he was safeguarding the limited but real apologetic value of his agreement with Christian philosophy while at the same time pro-tecting the truth of his own philosophy by keeping to this side of the limit beyond which he did not want to go. The same entreaty is ceaselessly recurring in his conversations with Catholic friends: "Do not make me say . . ."; "Say whatever you please so long as it is clear that you are speaking in your own name, but leave me out on this point. . . ." There is something pathetic in his words to Father Sertillanges: "You know I have no method to rise to that theology." And indeed, when it is a question of theology, the first prerequisite for the very possibility of any method is faith.

Not to have faith is not a personal fault, it is a misfortune; but the more a philosophy naturally agrees with the inspiration of a Christian philosophy, the more difficult it is for it not to look incomplete unless it expressly appeals to the Christian revelation. It seems to be aiming at a goal it is unable to reach. Believers find it hard to place themselves in the state of mind of those who have no faith. Bergson was so purely a philosopher in this respect that even the deepest agreements between his own thought and the teachings of Christian philosophy resembled more the chance encounters of two men whose paths happened to cross than the mutual understanding of two traveling companions. Bergson advanced very far within the truth of Christian philosophy. The further he went, the more conscious he became of an intimate harmony between his conception of the world and that of Christianity, but his awareness of this fact was for him the effect of an *intelligo ut credam* rather than that of a *credo ut intelligam*. He himself marveled all the more at this agreement since he had done nothing to bring it about. Whichever way he considered the problem, Bergson saw no other religion possible for him than Catholicism, but one can adhere to Catholicism only by faith and faith is not found at the conclusion of any philosophical reasoning.

For the further development of his philosophy there was at this point an obstacle which, in the order of pure nature, nothing could help Bergson to overcome.

It is not enough to say that Bergson had no faith. He did not even know what it was. I mean by this that he never suspected the meaning of the word in a Christian theology. As a philosopher, and he was nothing else, Bergson had a clear notion of the two types of knowledge, that of intelligence, of which science is the purest expression, and that of intuition, akin to instinct, which rises to awareness of itself in metaphysics. If someone spoke to him about faith, Bergson could not imagine that a third kind of knowledge was intended. In such cases, what he thought of corresponded roughly to the notion of obedience to Law, which precisely he was rejecting. To assent to a body of doctrinal positions to be accepted as true although they escaped both intelligence and intuition, and to do so solely on the strength of an external authority, this was something which our philosopher could not do. Not only did he never do it, but I have often wondered how those who were hoping for it could visualize what would have been for Bergson the day after his conversion. This philosopher, so careful in matters of philosophical assertion and who would not write one sentence without weighing its terms, would suddenly have had to meet the exigencies of dialecticians whose Thomism was more exacting than safe. I shall not give the devil the pleasure of making me name them. It would be all the more useless since, even without them, the adherence of Bergson to the Church would have implied on his part an act of global assent to a body of dogmas of which he knew too little to accept without further information. No doubt an implicit act of faith in the teachings of the

Church would have solved the problem. But, precisely, an assent of this sort was what could be least expected from him. Obedience has no place in philosophy. Faith comes to intelligence as a light that overflows it with joy and inspires it with a certitude that does away with questions.

A second limitation hampering Bergson's thought in his quest for truth was a certain lack of metaphysical disposition. One can do without it even in philosophy, but not if, as was Bergson's case, one is bent upon solving problems in the field of first philosophy. Here again Father Sertillanges was right. "Absence of metaphysics," "lack of metaphysics," these expressions and similar ones correctly describe the situation. I do not feel like subscribing to the somewhat rhetorical sentence of the same judge: "Face to face with positivism, Bergson acknowledged defeat." No, Bergson did not capitulate before positivism; the problem never arose in his mind. For my own part, I shall always refuse to confuse with one another two notions as different as positivism and the love of scientifically demonstrated conclusions. Bergson never denied the possibility of metaphysical knowledge, and he himself was eager to acquire it; but it remains true to say that, taking the word literally, he had no taste for a meta-physics floating in a stratosphere of abstractions completely cut off from all contact with physics. The fault with Bergson in this matter was not to despise metaphysics, not even not to have cultivated it, it was rather to have misunderstood its method. Bergson hoped to find it in a kind of empiricism based on an experience proper to metaphysics, entirely different from that of science and which nevertheless would lead to certitudes comparable with those of physics. The combination of these two errors, or rather the multiplication of one by the other, was to bring about disastrous results when the time arrived for him to come to grips with the problem of God.

The twenty-five years that Bergson spent in silence between *Creative Evolution* and *The Two Sources of Morality and Religion* were for him a time of intense meditation. There is no evidence that he ever questioned his competence to approach the problem, but his confidence in himself rested upon the very reason that should have made him hesitate. The notion of the God of religion hardly appeared in *Creative Evolution;* this time, on the contrary, the philosopher was about to enter the domain of Christian theology, and theologians felt entitled to call him to account. Bergson was willing to oblige, provided that it was only a philosophical account. In approaching problems so different from those he had hitherto studied, the philosopher did not for one minute consider altering his method. No doubt he would now have to draw on the experience of others and to speak of certain facts from hearsay; he would be called upon to broaden the basis of his empiricism so as to include the religious experience of the great mystics, but it still would be an empiricism adapted to the exigencies of religious facts.

I do not know what results such a method would yield were it applied to any other religion than Christianity. The problem of the very possibility of a philosophy of religion is here at stake. Unfortunately the considered admiration of Bergson for the Christian religion, and more precisely for Catholicism, was such that he did not hesitate to single out the great Catholic mystics as typical representatives of the religious experiences whose value he intended to assess. Having to philosophize about Christianity he did not have the least temptation to avoid Jesus Christ. After this it was

164

easy to foretell that the method would fail. Christianity is essentially a religion of the supernatural, and Catholic mysticism cannot be understood apart from the notion of grace. To discard these notions for reasons of methodology is to eliminate the very object of research. The Catholic mystic himself sees his own spiritual life as the working of grace in him. If he is wrong, the philosopher who submits this experience to his own scrutiny is philosophizing about an illusion without any other interest than a psychological one; if, on the contrary, the mystic is right, an objective study of his experience by the philosopher should first take into account the reality of grace and the supernatural order. A stranger to the Christian faith, ignoring the supernatural order as extraneous to the domain of philosophy, Bergson nevertheless attempted a philosophical interpretation of a religion in which everything is supernatural and grace. Up to this moment Bergson had found himself in a situation similar to that of Aristotle philosophizing on nature and discovering in the cosmos itself the presence of its first cause. This could be done in complete ignorance of any religious revelation. With *The Two Sources,* however, he became this strange hybrid: an Aristotle informed of the existence of Christianity, acquainted by personal study with the life and teaching of its Founder and saints, and attempting an interpretation of it after observing it from without as if it were but one more aspect of natural reality.

When I decided at last to read the book, I found my worst fears justified. For the first time, but beyond doubt, Bergson was handling reality against the grain. The method did not fit the object. Even genius served by intense research and inspired with the most generous sympathy will not suffice to make possible a natural theology of the supernatural life. The theologians who told him so were entirely right. Inasmuch as it pretends to apply to such Christian saints as Teresa of Avila or John of the Cross, the method of Bergson has no object. It is noteworthy that he himself never suspected it. Keeping faith with the spirit of his philosophy, which was "to be a true evolutionism and, consequently, a true prolongation of science," he failed to realize that a natural Christian mysticism was a contradiction in terms. One can prolong as far as one pleases the rational interpretation of nature without ever reaching the supernatural.

But Bergson himself had pondered on the problem longer than is commonly believed. I had an entirely unexpected proof of it on the occasion of the only prolonged and intimate interview I had with him and which, incidentally, he himself had provoked because he knew I desired it. It took place at the Maison Rouge in Strasbourg when, after the liberation of Alsace, he brought Alsatians his homage. The lecture he had given at the University was in substance the one he had already given in 1913 to the Society for Psychical Research of London. I did not think then that there could be any relation between the unusual subject matter of this lecture, in which he dealt with cases of telepathy that he held for certain although he admitted to no experience of them, and the turn he gave to our conversation. There was one, however, and a very deep one, but, at that date, how could I suspect it?

After a few words on the history of medieval philosophy, Bergson asked me point-blank: "Why do you not direct your research toward the philosophy of religion? You are the man to handle this problem and, as I believe, with a good chance of success." What a proposal! Philosophy and religion together, all at once, for a young apprentice still in the process of getting acquainted with his own theology, and, moreover, a proposal coming from Bergson who, so far, had given no indication that he was interested in this problem. In those days many a young man could speak bergsonese fluently without having to look for his words. In the seconds of silence that followed two ideas flashed through my mind: religious life at the most advanced point of creative evolution; the institutions and dogmas of Christianity left behind by this spiritual energy as its material by-products. Obviously this would not do. Catholicism would always refuse to recognize itself under this simplified scheme. I could not hesitate on the answer to give: "Why would you not undertake such a piece of research yourself? It requires no lesser a philosopher than you." Bergson answered with a smile, slightly lingering on the last words: "Descartes did not very much like to publish his thoughts in matters of morals and religion. He wanted to preserve his peace of mind . . ." We laughed. We had understood each other. The offer of this perilous mission was not renewed.

Thus, at least thirteen years before the publication of *The Two Sources,* Bergson had already come to grips with this immense problem and he was inviting me to run the risk, apparently unaware that no philosophical method was qualified to cope with an order of facts which, because it depended directly on the divine initiative, could be competently handled only by theology. Bergson wanted to reach Christian mysticism by following the *élan vital* upstream to its source, and even, if necessary, somewhat beyond; but the very essence of the Christian mystical life was that it came entirely from above as a gratuitous gift. That the philosophy of Bergson remained to the end a naturalism can scarcely be doubted. Whatever in this religion of the *élan vital* transcends the order of nature still belongs within nature. Bergsonian religious knowledge does not succeed philosophical knowledge as, in Christianity, faith perfects reason but, rather, as probability prolongs certitude. While reading the conclusions of *The Two Sources,* I understood at last how the lecture given at Strasbourg on psychic phenomena was indeed related to our ensuing conversation about religion. Bergson was expecting from these sciences nothing less than the experimental proof of the existence of an order of spiritual realities.

Observing this great mind at work seeking, by way of nature and reason, an entrance to the supernatural world that only faith could provide, one remembers the words of Saint Thomas speaking of the efforts of philosophers to solve the loftiest theological problems by way of philosophy: "One sees thereby in what great straits these brilliant geniuses found themselves. . . ." Henri Bergson was one of them; he had gone through their *angustias,* those tortures of a mind confined in an enclosure without exit. Bergson has spoken a great deal since his death. The more carefully we read the words attributed to him, the less they invite us to suppose that he ever gave up the philosophism that inspired all his writings. If in the secret of his heart, our master finally saw a higher light, the miracle came too late to benefit his doctrine. Far from seeing in *The Two Sources* the point of Bergson's nearest approach to Christianity, I am rather inclined to see in this work the symbol of the inability of his philosophy to reach the level of the Christian religion.

Nevertheless it was in this very field of philosophy that Bergson was to make up for his failure. Circumstances were hardly favorable. Neoscholasticism was slumbering and repeating itself. The arrival of Berg-

sonism was for it an excellent occasion to manifest the
power of renovation and perennial fecundity of Christian wisdom; but instead of assuming Bergson as Saint
Thomas had assumed Aristotle, it would almost seem
(incredibly enough) that it was afraid of him. Scholastics wasted their time in refuting him, instead of
extracting from his works the truth they contained. Yet,
owing to Saint Thomas, there was no need for us to
create any new metaphysics. Had a single one of us
understood that Christian philosophy was at last finding
its chance, he would not have been satisfied with opposing to the *élan vital* the static god of Aristotle,
nor on the contrary to let the Christian God drift along
with the flux of Bergsonian becoming. It was enough
to restore to His place of pride the Pure Act of Being,
the I AM of Scripture and the God of Thomism, Who
transcends the finite categories of the static and the
dynamic, the immobile and the mobile, the ready-made
and the self-making, in short, the being and the becoming, in order to extract from the new philosophy
the precious nugget of gold it contained. Let us not
forget that according to Saint Thomas himself, God
is above even being (*ens*) because He is *esse*. But it
must be said that, at that time, most people had forgotten the Act, the essence of which is to be, purely
and simply. This at least is certain: of those who took
Bergson to task, not one seems to have remembered
that truth.

An extraordinary thing then came to pass. Thomism
had not known how to give Bergsonism what it needed
to reach its own truth, but Bergsonism then began to
move as if it was groping in the Christian philosophy
of Saint Thomas for the truths it needed. A sure instinct led it there, for no Christian disciple of Bergson
could resign himself to believe that the Bergsonian

169

victory over modern materialism should be left unexploited. At the end of its course, Bergsonism had in its possession at least a few truths that the decaying Thomism of those who rebuked him was sometimes lacking; but since the Church could not err in her choice of a Common Doctor, the Thomism of Saint Thomas himself could not not be able to do justice to these truths. Christian philosophy then resumed for a time its pilgrimage, but this time it was a pilgrimage to its own source. Under the guidance of Clio, she returned to it as to the fountain of youth.

Two events marked this quest. The first was the thesis, *The Intellectualism of Saint Thomas*, defended in the Sorbonne by Father Pierre Rousselot, S.J. This took place in 1908; its author could not then have undergone the influence of *Creative Evolution*, and I do not even know if the two previous books of Bergson were in any way at the origin of his reflections. At any rate, it is certain that in this memorable thesis Father Rousselot was the first one to bring back to its rightful place the Thomistic notion of intelligence conceived as the source and cause of the discursive operations of reason. One could not understand the import of this conclusion without seeing at once the error of Bergson. Its origin was now visible. Under the name of intelligence, Bergson had simply brought reason to trial.

It is from that time that some Thomists began to retrace their steps to the notion of intelligence as the master himself understood it. Some later went very far in that direction, and there was indeed a long way to go. The scholastic interlocutors of Bergson themselves had lost the meaning of this key notion; for the intellectualism of Saint Thomas they had simply substituted their own rationalism. The rediscovery of the genuine meaning of the word "intellect" in the doctrine of the master opened a new way for a more flexible and more comprehensive theory of knowledge. It is only too true that a certain rationalism, which is hostile to the intellect, is characterized by a natural inability to understand life, and precisely the one facing Bergson was of that kind. It was the kind of scholastic reason that does not remember its intellectual essence. True reason is the simple light of intellect which, in order to investigate reality, diffracts itself into various rational movements. There is not a single Thomistic theory of knowledge today that has not absorbed the conclusions of the criticism directed by Bergson against the rationalism of Spencer and Taine. Those among us who rather bitterly reproach Bergson with his notion of an intuition akin to instinct and opposed to intelligence, currently speak of an intellectual intuition conceived as able to fulfill all the operations attributed by Bergson to intuition and quite particularly as being itself a light and a life and therefore able to grasp life in its very essence. The intellectualism of such Thomists has devoured Bergsonian intuition. Doctrines of this sort owe their more genuine intellectualism to the effort they were forced to make in order to understand the Bergsonian criticism of the intellect for the very error it was.

The second one of these events was the rediscovery, made by some Thomists familiar with the work of Bergson, of the authentic meaning of the two notions of being and God such as it would seem today that Saint Thomas himself understood them. Contrary to what some consider evident, contemporary existentialism played no part in this affair. It is Saint Thomas who made us read Kierkegaard and not the reverse. One must really be ignorant of the true nature of the issue to imagine that a better understanding of Saint Thomas can be derived from Kierkegaard, whom he had outdistanced even before he was born. In fact, Thomism is ahead of what all future philosophies may say about being and God. But this is true only of the God of Saint Thomas, Whose absolute transcendence in the order of being sets Him once and for all beyond all conceivable limits. The natural theologies of the present and the future can rest assured that in reaching its term each one of them will still see ahead this pillar of fire; all it will do will be to offer it one more object to illuminate.

Bergsonism was no exception to the rule. It did not have within itself the power to rise to the Christian God, but when the intimations of truth which it brought with it met Christian philosophy within Christian minds they somehow raised themselves to its summit, as if moved by the only force that could carry them to their fulfillment. For some of us, at least, this was one of the origins of their rediscovery of the true notion of being. It is an error to see this event as a contamination of Thomism by Bergsonism. On the contrary, it was a decontamination of schoolroom Thomism disfigured and robbed of its efficacy by the proliferation of adventitious theologies. Bergson did not convert us to Bergsonism, nor did he convert us to Thomism, nor still did he induce us to bergsonify Saint Thomas; rather, by sobering our minds of the aftermath of an excess of abstraction, he enabled us to hear in the words of Saint Thomas some essential truths of Christian philosophy to which his own doctrine was attuned. The philosophy of Bergson has made it easier for us to approach the authentic God of Saint Thomas.

This is the only revenge that Bergson exacted on us who proved so inexpert in the art of being Thomists.

This unexpected handmaid unwittingly contributed her stone to the building of the tower. By awakening us from our rationalist slumber in order to call us to the life of intelligence, Bergson made it possible for us to enter more deeply into our own truth.

CHRISTIAN PHILOSOPHY

The Catholics who came to grips with these difficulties during the first half of the twentieth century retain from those days the feeling that they lived in the midst of an extreme confusion. A key notion was lacking, that of theology. They know it today, too late to have benefited by its light, and with the single consolation that someone will some day be able to put it to good use.

Warning signs were not lacking, but for unknown reasons Catholic philosophers did not heed them. Among the acts that Pope Leo XIII listed as the principal ones of his reign on the occasion of the twenty-fifth anniversary of his election, he placed first the encyclical *Aeterni Patris*, given in Rome on the fourth of August, 1879. This document traditionally has the following heading: *On the Restoration in Catholic Schools of Christian Philosophy According to the Mind of the Angelic Doctor Saint Thomas Aquinas*. The great encyclicals which followed, including the programs of social reform, presuppose as accomplished this first intellectual reform as the necessary condition of all the others. And yet what vagrant teacher has not experienced it twenty times? If he is asked to speak of the social programs of Leo XIII, he would be ill-advised to begin with *Aeterni Patris!* What people want is something practical, such as *Rerum Novarum* on the condition of workers and employers, for instance. And yet short cuts will not save time. He who does not enter the problem by the gate of Christian philosophy is sure to go astray. Some have done it and their successors are still with us.

It is not that the encyclical *Aeterni Patris* has fallen into oblivion. On the contrary, supported by other pontifical acts and, of course, widely publicized by Thomists of all persuasions, this letter has never ceased to be read, translated, and commented on. Volumes specially dedicated to its study have been published, but it is interesting to observe that the attention of the commentators has focused by preference on the conclusion of the encyclical and, quite precisely, on the page in which the Pope ordered Catholic schools to conform their philosophical and theological teaching to the doctrine of Saint Thomas. Thomists were pleased, others considered themselves exempted, and still others claimed that they had complied with the rule before it was laid down. It seemed evident to everyone that such was indeed the point and substance of the pontifical message, the rest being there to fill out the document and sugar-coat the pill. Concerning the notion of Christian philosophy, we neither heard nor read any commentary at the time of the modernist crisis. It would seem that no one was interested in it.

This notion was nonetheless one of the most certain origins of *Aeterni Patris*. Forgotten in 1907 when it survived only in the title of a philosophical review, it had been very much alive in the years immediately preceding 1879. One no longer reads the famous lenten sermons given by Ventura de Raulica, whose name I have already mentioned. Never was there a more total devotion to the truth of the Church, never a more ardent admiration for Saint Thomas and his work. "Saint Thomas, brethren, what a man! What a genius! He is human reason itself raised to its highest. Beyond the efforts of his reasoning is the vision of heavenly things." While reading these lines, one cannot help remembering the more modest view that Saint Thomas took of the *Summa Theologiae:* "To me it looks like straw." Ventura did not feel that way: "The *Summa*," he said, "is a most stupendous book, the deepest, the most marvelous ever written by the hand of man; for Holy Scripture came from the hand of God." And yet this vigorous attack by Father Ventura on the philosophical rationalism inherited from the eighteenth century by his age was itself linked to what can be called the opposite error, namely, the very traditionalism which, as has been seen, wanted everything to rest upon revelation, even reason. Rome decided that the question needed to be clarified. Although fairly recent, the notion of Christian philosophy had its value. It obviously corresponded to a reality; it could not be allowed to disappear. On the other hand it was important that it should be dissociated from traditionalism in which it had become involved. For if philosophy itself is one of the varieties of revelation, only Scripture and tradition remain. The encyclical of 1879 had for one of its aims a clarification of the notion of Christian philosophy. After this needed purification, the notion could be safely used.

Once more I am indebted to Clio for having rediscovered, at a much later date, this notion then fallen into disuse among philosophers. In 1931 and 1932, the Gifford Lectures provided an unexpected opportunity to define the *Spirit of Mediaeval Philosophy*. It was not a question of describing this philosophy, supposed to be a single philosophy, commonly called "scholasticism" and considered to be the common teaching of all the Doctors of the middle ages. The study of Christian thought was already too far advanced for anyone to entertain such an illusion. One could not imagine that Saint Anselm, Saint Thomas Aquinas, Saint Bonaventure, John Duns Scotus, and William of Ockham had all taught one and the same philosophy. On the other hand, it was obvious enough that, although their philosophies and as a consequence their theologies were different, these masters all agreed on the truth of the Christian revelation received by faith. They thus reached the same religious truth by different philosophical ways, and this fundamental agreement contributed to conferring a kind of unity upon the whole of these doctrines, not only as to the letter of their conclusions but also as to their spirit. The only conceivable cause of this harmony is their Christian character. Different as philosophies, for their surface Aristotelianism hardly concealed deep-seated divergences, these doctrines were united by the Christian spirit that inspired them. Whatever unity they had came to them, as to their form, from the Aristotelian technique that they all used, but, as to the doctrinal substance, from religion rather than from philosophy. A forgotten formula was available to describe this way of philosophizing: the spirit of medieval philosophy was that of "Christian philosophy."

I felt somewhat embarrassed to have to characterize the philosophy of the middle ages by a formula of which the history of that philosophy provided practically no example. Indeed, a master in theology teaching in the thirteenth century would never have considered himself as having a philosophy, even a Christian one. The title of theologian, of which he felt proud, suited him perfectly. It was no longer so in 1907. The philosophism that had accumulated since the seventeenth century had outmoded the type of speculation proper to the era heralded by Lactantius, when all philosophers would be priests. Victor Cousin had drawn the logical conclusion when he said in his famous course of 1818: "The philosophy that preceded Descartes actually was theology." It was on this occasion that he wrote the words we have borrowed from him: "The philosophy of Descartes is the separation of philosophy and theology." Coming from him, this was a compliment. De Gerando had preceded him on this road when, in 1808, he wrote in his *Comparative History of Philosophical Systems:* "It was then that philosophy began to separate itself from theology, and had the good fortune, thanks to this divorce, to become again a secular study." One century later, to speak of Christian philosophy was enough to suggest the idea of a remarriage after a divorce that philosophy did not seem to regret. And yet what other name could one find for this body of doctrines so deeply marked with the seal of the Christian religion? Since indeed such a large portion of it was so truly rational that modern philosophy had appropriated it, one could rightly call it a philosophy, and since this philosophy was quickened by a genuinely Christian spirit, there was no escape from calling it a "Christian" philosophy.

This was done and the result was a lively controversy. What was at stake was a label. The two opposing factions did not divide as could have been predicted. The notion of Christian philosophy had as its opponents unbelievers as well as Catholic philosophers, priests, and religious of all denominations. There was even a philosopher advocating a philosophy that could rightly call itself Catholic, such as was his own philosophy, but not Christian. I myself had used it as a handy label to designate a group of facts whose reality could not be denied, but the theologians wanted to take apart the mechanism that made it possible for faith to collaborate with reason, and vice versa, without either one losing its essence. However, a fundamental opposition persisted during all the ups and downs of the quarrel. Since the facts themselves were granted, this verbal dispute was bound to peter out, as it did in the minds of most of the debaters. In the meantime I, who had imprudently provoked it, was trying to understand the origins of such a controversial formula. I then made the discovery that fifty years before, Pope Leo XIII had written the encyclical *Aeterni Patris* to clear up its meaning.

I had never read it? No, never, and I confess it to my own confusion, but history ordinarily follows the line of the likely, which is that of the novel, rather than the line of the true, which it claims for its own. It should be known too, that in those days, philosophers were not frequent readers of papal encyclicals. This remark may still be partly true. The Church is not unaware of it, but she bides her time, knowing that one day philosophers will read them when they feel the need.

The first contact with encyclicals is not easy. The difficulty is not that they are written in a chancery Latin adorned with humanistic elegances of style; the difficulty is rather that the exact meaning of the doctrine is not always easily grasped. In order to find it one then undertakes to translate them and, in so doing, one finally understands the reason for their style. One cannot replace the words of this pontifical Latin by others borrowed from any one among the great modern literary languages, and still less rephrase these sentences differently without at once realizing that, however carefully this is done, the original loses some of its force in the process; and not only some of its force, but some of its precision as well. But this is not the whole of the difficulty. The true difficulty, well known to those who have tried it, is to respect scrupulously what can be called, without any paradox, the precision of its imprecisions—the carefully calculated precision of its intentional imprecisions. More than once we have the feeling, after some reflection, that on a certain point we know exactly what the encyclical means, but it does not say so expressly, and without doubt it has good grounds not to be more precise. Such documents are equally eloquent in what they say and in what they do not exclude. After the course in theology they greatly need, and which would require several years, it would be profitable for Christian philosophers to attend for a time a finishing school located somewhere between the Lateran and the Vatican, and preferably attached to the Gregorian, where they would be taught the art of reading a papal encyclical.

This is a subtle art, with no necessary link with metaphysics. For instance, does the encyclical *Aeterni Patris* deal with the notion of "Christian philosophy?" Yes, since the very words are included in the title. Granted, but the title of an encyclical is no part of the encyclical; it does not carry the guarantee of papal infallibility. If it did, how could we explain that, being included in the title, the expression is nowhere to be found in the text? True enough, the same Pope freely used it elsewhere, but in documents less solemn and, at any rate, not the one in which it should be, according to the title, one of the main topics. One then begins to wonder. Hearing Christians of great zeal and good will, but dangerously confused in their talk, speak of Christian philosophy, did not the great pontiff deem it opportune to put some order in their minds? They had to be told, then, what Christian philosophy was. This is what the title announces. From then on the formula ceases to be suspect; the specter of traditionalism and of fideism which haunted it has just been exorcised. It then becomes possible for anyone to speak of Christian philosophy provided he understands by these words the way of philosophizing described in the encyclical. Yet the Pope does not introduce the formula in the body itself of the encyclical letter, because his proper object is to define a certain way of philosophizing which it prescribes and not the use of some particular name to designate it, which remains an open question. Included in the letter, the expression would have become compulsory, whereas the Church has done without it for so many centuries that even today she should still be able to do without it. Let none therefore try either to impose or to forbid its use; what is important is that, if it is used, it should be used correctly.

An encyclical is an essentially religious act, prompted by religious motives and aiming at a religious purpose. It is therefore certain that one would look in it in vain for instruction concerning the manner of philosophizing proper to minds without faith in a supernatural revelation. It is legitimate for philosophers to make that remark, but this does not justify their refusal to take into consideration philosophical teaching conceived in a Christian spirit. When conclusions are offered as philosophical, they should be examined as such. The origin of an idea does not affect its value. A philosopher can speculate on the basis of a myth, or a religious belief, or a dream, or a personal emotional experience, or a social group experience, it does not matter; what his reason makes of it is what counts. In any case, it remains certain that the teaching of *Aeterni Patris*, an act of the ordinary magisterial authority of the Church, is religious in both inspiration and aim.

It is worthy of note that the Pope did not attempt a doctrinal synthesis of the kind of philosophy that can be called "Christian." This should be a lesson to certain theologians overfond of definitions. Pronounce the words "Christian philosophy" and they will immediately insist upon obtaining from you a definition of its essence. They want to know *that which* Christian philosophy is. If you thoughtlessly defer to their request, they will at once seize this bone of contention and lose interest in everything else. Do not attempt either to offer them a historical description instead of a definition, for they would accuse you of historicism, an epithet whose meaning is somewhat hazy but which never portends anything good. Now precisely in this encyclical on the duty to restore or re-establish Christian philosophy in the Catholic schools, pagan, Jewish, or Protestant schools are not involved. The Pope gives no definition of what he himself understands by Christian philosophy. In fact, as has been said, the formula appears nowhere in the body of the letter, but nothing is more significant than this absence for those who understand the reason for it. Whatever the reason for its presence in the title, the reason for its absence from the encyclical is clear enough. In pontifical chancery style, this silence means that the Church does not forbid the use of the expression and even that, under certain conditions, she favors it. If one understands by these words the manner of philosophizing described in the encyclical, the formula is legitimate but not necessary. The proof is that the encyclical itself does very well without it. In short, provided the Christian philosophizes in the manner described in the encyclical, it matters little whether his philosophy is called Christian or not. The formula is permitted, not prescribed.

This does not matter, it will be said. Since in the title of the letter the Pope spoke of "Christian philosophy according to the mind of Saint Thomas Aquinas," he obviously made no distinction between Christian philosophy and the philosophy of Saint Thomas.

Once more this would be reaching a hasty conclusion. The encyclical does not say: "Christian philosophy, that is to say, the philosophy of Thomas Aquinas" (*christiana philosophia, id est* or *sive philosophia divi Thomae Aquinatis*). Nothing was easier to say, and if the letter does not say it, the reason is that it wants to say something else. But what does it want to say? Translations of the Latin word *mens* are many. The difficulty is to choose one not distorting the intention of the author. This cannot be a question of the manner in which Saint Thomas conceived Christian philosophy, since he never spoke of it. One should not say according to the *idea* Saint Thomas had of it, for the same reason. *In the spirit of* Saint Thomas, an easy and acceptable translation, should not be rejected, although it may mislead in suggesting that Saint Thomas had a personal manner of conceiving this notion, which, as we said above, is not the case. Tentatively, I would suggest as the most conservative translation: *in agreement with the thought of* Saint Thomas Aquinas. Assuredly it is simpler not to translate, and the English word matters little provided it does not lead the mind astray. Whichever English word be chosen, its intention should be to signify the authentic meaning of the Latin word *mens* in the pontifical document itself. It is necessary to be clear on this point if one wants to interpret the document correctly. Now the word itself seems to signify the manner of thinking personal to Saint Thomas, including, of course, what he himself is thinking when he philosophizes as a Christian.

We are now nearing our conclusion; let us not be shipwrecked in sight of the harbor. For at the last moment there comes to mind as an irresistible temptation an honest and direct translation: according to the *doctrine* of Saint Thomas. Nothing forbids it. In the last analysis this even is what the title really says: how to re-establish or restore, in Catholic schools, the doctrine of Saint Thomas. No doubt, but such is not the direct and immediate meaning of the encyclical in which, in any case, no definition of the doctrine of Saint Thomas

Aquinas is to be found. There is there no abstract definition, of which no doctrine is susceptible, nor even
any analytical listing of the chief theses one should
hold in order to be faithful to the teaching of Saint
Thomas, so that to reject one of them would amount
to rejecting the doctrine itself. Such a listing has been
attempted since, with no other result than to create
new sources of controversy. I do not deny that the
attempt is legitimate. My point is simply that Leo XIII
himself did not do it in his encyclical *Aeterni Patris*,
from which it can reasonably be inferred that such was
not the object of this doctrinal act. Christian philosophy
is not directly identified with any body of specific doctrines, but it remains that, not excluding possible and
even foreseeable ulterior determinations, the primary
intention of the title of the encyclical prescribes that
the teaching of Catholic schools should follow a philosophy that conforms to the thought of Saint Thomas
and, in the first place, to the way he himself understood
philosophical speculation. This at least the encyclical
has defined in terms as precise as possible. Let us observe now how the definition has been prepared.

The competence of the Holy See in matters of philosophy is related to its apostolic mission. When saying
to his apostles (Matt. 28:19), "Going therefore, teach
ye all nations," Jesus Christ left the Church he had
founded the common and universal teacher of the nations. Whichever way it be conceived, therefore, Christian philosophy will be linked with the teaching function
of the Church. It will even be so as a matter of primary
purpose, for philosophy has often been a source of
error. It is against vain philosophy that the Apostle
warned the faithful (Coloss. 2:8), and this is also the
reason why, while working with all their might to en-
courage a learning worthy of the name of science, the

popes have zealously seen to it "that all studies should accord with the Catholic faith, especially philosophy on which a right interpretation of the other sciences in great part depends"; and not only the interpretation of the sciences but likewise the conduct of societies. The deep thought of Leo XIII is announced at the beginning of the encyclical, and it is a social thought, given that the order of all society rests on the knowledge of truth accepted by those who govern the body politic. The Christian religion, spread by the teaching of the faith in the entire world, is alone able to teach the truth and nothing but the truth. Still, one should not neglect the natural aids that the divine wisdom has devised to facilitate the work of faith. The main one is "the right use of philosophy. For, not in vain did God set the light of reason in the human mind; and so far is the super-added light of faith from extinguishing or lessening the power of the intelligence that it completes it rather, and by adding to its strength renders it capable of greater things."

The problem at stake in *Aeterni Patris*, then, is, at a time of social unrest, itself caused by intellectual confusion, to appeal to human learning to set nations back again on the road to salvation. However one may feel about the notion of "Christian philosophy," this much is certain from the outset that it should define an apostolic use of philosophy, conceived as an auxiliary to the work of redemption. But whereas one was expecting to be told what truth this philosophy teaches, one sees it call on witnesses to attest its antiquity in the tradition of the Church. Leo XIII thus resorts to the testimony of history. However, this abridged history of Christian philosophy will tacitly but continually refer to the teaching of Saint Thomas in his *Summa*

Theologiae and beyond Saint Thomas to Saint Augustine.

The body of the encyclical, consequently, is a history of the use that the Fathers of the Church and ecclesiastical writers have made of philosophy, from the first century of the Church, to help propagate the faith, beginning with the establishment of its preambles, that is to say, the saving truth that the natural reason is able to know. The body of these truths constitutes what many theologians, philosophers, or masters in scholastic philosophy today call the "natural theology" of Saint Thomas Aquinas; and indeed, if he had one, this was it. One can think of nothing else to put under this name. But if we suppose this philosophical activity of the natural reason to be free from all attachment to revelation, we shall be mistaken. On this point, everyone should weigh with precision the words of the encyclical: "And, assuredly, the God of all goodness, in all that pertains to divine things, has not only manifested by the light of faith those truths which human intelligence could not attain of itself, but others, also, not altogether unattainable by reason (*nunnullas . . . rationi non omnino impervias*), that by the help of divine authority they may be made known to all at once and without any admixture of error." The teaching of the *Summa* shines through the text of the encyclical. Even for the revealed truths accessible to the human reason and of which philosophy can know something, it is appropriate to say only that these are not entirely inaccessible to it. That which is *non omnino impervium* is not exactly *pervium*. Moreover the added weight of God's authority is needed to make this "not-altogether-inaccessible" be known at once (from the age of reason), by all (and not by philosophers only) and without any admixture of errors. This amounts to saying that every time divine things are at stake (God and all knowledge necessary for salvation) no one can pretend to reach truth unless he relies upon revelation to safeguard him against error.

At this point, close and strong ties between philosophy and revelation are effected. For it thus comes to pass that truths proposed by God to be believed, or closely related to the teaching of faith, have been known by the wise men of antiquity through the sole light of natural reason as well as demonstrated and defended by them. The pagan philosophers have given expression to some truth—*quaedam vera*—and even though these were at times mingled with error, it still is worth while to put these fragments of truth in the service of revelation, in showing through facts that, on the testimony of its adversaries, human wisdom is a witness in favor of faith. One cannot read the encyclical without thinking that the domain in which this collaboration takes place should have limits, since it includes only the truths related to God and human salvation that natural reason is able to understand. But it is appropriate to emphasize how intimate and wide this collaboration is, extending as it does even to philosophical doctrines of pagan origin, provided these be linked by close ties—*arctis quibusdam vinculis*—to the teaching of the faith. Thus did the Fathers of the Church, Greek or Latin, make use of philosophy: Aristides, Justin, Irenaeus, Origen, the two Gregories, Basil, and Augustine.

The conclusion of this part of the encyclical should be noted with care, since it is a stumbling block for so many philosophers, Christian or otherwise: "But if natural reason first sowed this rich field of doctrine before it was rendered fruitful by the power of Christ, it must assuredly become more prolific after the grace of the Saviour has renewed and added to the native faculties of the human mind. And who does not see that a plain and easy road is opened up to faith by such a method of philosophic study?" *Hoc philosophandi genus:* what is at stake is truly a philosophical use of reason, but one that nevertheless refuses to do without the light of faith, places itself in the service of revelation and its ends, is in return restored and increased by the words of Christ and thereby rendered still more fruitful. I apologize for insisting on the point, but it should be clear that, in all this, the encyclical speaks of the enrichment of natural reason taken precisely *qua* natural. Let us, speaking under our own responsibility, interpret it as meaning a natural reason raised to the state of grace. The remarkable discoveries we owe Saint Thomas Aquinas in metaphysics, cosmogony, anthropology, and ethics are so many proofs of the enrichment natural reason can receive from the grace of God.

There is more. This same manner of philosophizing has other advantages. Since I mentioned the Latin of encyclical letters, I beg to note that, so far, the document has achieved this remarkable feat: it has not given a name to the exercise of reason under discussion. The Pope has named it neither theology nor philosophy, nor even Christian philosophy. There is such a thing as philosophy, but it is not here under discussion. Since the *philosophia* Leo XIII has in mind is that which reason uses in the service of revelation, this use can be, of itself, neither revelation nor philosophy. It is, our Latin says, the right use of philosophy—*rectum philosophiae usum.* It is also called a certain way of philosophizing—*hujusmodi philosophandi genus.* It can even be something rather hard to translate: a *philosophandi institutum,* the deliberate resolve to philosophize in that particular way. Whatever name we choose, what is at stake is always a reason philosophizing in intimate union with faith, in a mutual exchange of benefits.

This does not mean that he who philosophizes in this manner should bar himself from approaching problems apparently considered as properly theological. It is not enough for it to demonstrate the existence of God; this way of philosophizing likewise establishes that God possesses all perfections and each one of them in its supreme degree: infinite wisdom, which nothing escapes, supreme justice, which no ill feeling can sway, so that it can be said of God not only that He is true, but that He is truth itself. Thus does human reason win to God the trust and obedience of men. Moreover a reason thus directed testifies in favor of the evangelical truth as attested by the miracles of Christ, and thereby declares that all those who believe in the Gospel do not do so lightly, as one believes in fables. Lastly, the same reason establishes that the Church has been founded by Christ as can be seen, the Vatican Council says, from its surprising propagation, its eminent holiness, its universal and inexhaustible fecundity, its unity, and its invincible stability. All this creates for the reason a great and perpetual motive of credibility, a lasting witness to the divine mission of the Church.

Thus understood, this way of philosophizing overflows on all sides the limits traditionally assigned to philosophy pure and simple. Ever attentive to the word of God, reason now leads the philosopher to the threshold of faith; indeed it proves that it is reasonable for man to submit his intelligence and his judgment to the authority of God; reason even proves that the Church was founded by Christ. Who, then, could fail to see what duties derive for us from the certainty of its divine institution? Here, however, this kind of philosophy reaches its limit. It will go no further because what is beyond escapes the grasp of reason. Then theology begins, but philosophy can still be of assistance. By using the methods and the help of philosophy, sacred theology will acquire the nature, structure, and spirit of a true science, that is, of a body of conclusions deduced from principles. Reason does still more. It procures a more accurate and richer knowledge of things pertaining to faith. This applies even to mysteries of which all the Fathers of the Church agree that reason can give us a "somewhat more lucid understanding, as far as it can go." To conclude, let us not forget the many services rendered to theology by reason in helping to preserve intact the treasures of revealed truth and in refuting the errors of its adversaries. Convinced that whatever contradicts the word of God is false, reason finds in this certitude courage and inspiration to turn against the enemies of faith their own weapons.

Why call a *genus philosophandi* a use of reason so different from that of the philosophers? Simply because the philosophizing that reason is here doing is indeed philosophy. It is philosophy itself that will bear this fruit provided it accepts the role of co-operating with revelation. In all that which falls under its competence, let philosophy follow its own method, use its own principles and its own methods of demonstration. Even in such matters, it should not want to withdraw itself from the divine authority which is its surest guarantee against error and increases its knowledge. This is where, as I believe, the encyclical says of this "philosophy," which is less a doctrine than a religious use of reason, the essentials of what it intended to say. In this religious use of reason, philosophy should be present such as it is in itself, or otherwise the Christian could not really use it. But this philosophy should also live in a kind of symbiosis with Christian faith: "Those, therefore, who to the study of philosophy unite obedience to the Christian faith, are philosophizing in the best possible way; for the splendor of the divine truths, received into the mind, helps the understanding, and not only detracts in nowise from its dignity, but adds greatly to its nobility, keenness, and stability."

The reading of the encyclical is enough to reveal how ignorant of the question were the philosophers and the theologians who engaged in a controversy on the notion of Christian philosophy between 1930 and 1940. As far as I can remember, it seems that all of them were looking for a definition of this notion by its form, essence, or quiddity. Naturally enough none was found. For if it is of the essence of philosophy to pursue the knowledge of causes in the light of the natural reason, and if, on the contrary, it is of the essence of theology to pursue the same quest in the light of supernatural revelation, then it is clearly impossible that one single discipline should share in the nature of both. Since the encyclical *Aeterni Patris* had been promulgated many years before, all the contestants should have known that what was at stake was, before anything else, a certain way to apply philosophical methods to the investigation of faith. Should one ask what is meant by this "certain way," the answer should be: first, that of the Fathers of the Church, then, that of the Scholastic Doctors. If one reads this sketch of the history of twelve centuries, he will not find in it one single name that is not the name of a theologian, and yet these names recall to our mind the works of men who greatly contributed to enriching the patrimony of philosophy: *patrimonium philosophiae plurimum locupletarunt.* If these words of Leo XIII needed confirmation, history would provide it. Far from coming after the Greeks almost as though there had been nothing between itself and the Greeks, the philosophy of the seventeenth century is inexplicable both in content and form if one does not take into consideration, along with the Jewish-Christian revelation, the fourteen centuries of theology which have relentlessly tried to achieve some understanding of the faith on which they were founded.

This use made of reason within faith and for it, but finally assuming the shape of a science, is exactly what is called scholasticism. In the history of Christian thought, especially if one compares it with the theology of the Fathers, scholasticism does not represent a new doctrine, but rather a new intellectual style corresponding to the time when, suddenly fed by the Aristotelian stream, the Christian tradition absorbed a mass of new philosophical and scientific notions. To find something similar in the past, one has to go back as far as Saint Basil, whose name evokes to the mind that of Saint Albert the Great, but whose Greek erudition did not bring about any change in the mode of exposition of Christian truth. As to Augustine, he had to assimilate Plotinus, but there was no science in Plotinus, there were only some metaphysics and ethics. On the contrary, a mere glance at the commentaries of Saint Thomas on Aristotle is enough to reveal the nature of the change that then took place. Christians then undertook something that was not in itself new, since Boethius had already attempted it though not on such a scale, namely, a study of philosophy in depth and in its manifold disciplines. Assuredly, this study was always undertaken with the same end in view: to co-operate with the work of redemption; but it required a specific effort, and it had a distinct proximate end, which was to learn philosophy and how to philosophize. In a series of means and ends, each means presents itself as a provisory end. In studying mathematics with a view to the study of physics, there is a moment when one must study mathematics as one would do if one pursued the subject for itself. One must learn Latin grammar as a grammarian would, even if it is to read Virgil. So, too, the masters of the middle ages had to philosophize as philosophers do because there was no other way to master philosophy in order to serve Christian truth usefully through it. They did so, with the result that the part of philosophical speculation in theology grew out of proportion to what was left for the study of Scripture, which is the center and heart of Christian learning.

The balance was still maintained in the thirteenth century. As a general rule, the masters who, like Albert and Thomas, made such a large use of philosophy, were not called "philosophers." Appropriately enough, this name was reserved for pagans and infidels given to the study of philosophy, while the Fathers of the Church and those who prolonged their tradition were called the "saints" (*sancti*). As to the representatives of the new style in theology, they were called the *philosophantes*, that is, those who "philosophize" in the study and teaching of the divine revelation. This swelling of the part allotted to philosophy made it necessary to study and to teach it in schools. This was done and the distinct discipline thus constituted as a consequence of this development became "scholastic philosophy." The most remarkable result of this event was that, as a counterpart to this scholastic philosophy, there was born a scholastic theology. One could almost say "theology" without any qualification, for though the word was traditional and known to all, there are only very few works written during the period from Saint Justin to Saint Thomas Aquinas in whose titles the word "theology" appears. So long as whatever was written was theology, no particular name was needed to designate it. Saint Thomas himself was not yet used to the change. For though the word "theology" is conspicuous in the title of his *Summa Theologiae,* it seldom appears in the body of the work. This suggests that a new use was being made of this ancient word.

It is essential to recall that scholastic philosophy did not change its nature when it separated itself from theology, but it was violently tempted to do so. Every undertaking has its own risks, but this one, often denounced by the theologians of the middle ages had been foreseen and deliberately accepted. Accidents did happen, some of them serious, but in denouncing the excessive use of philosophy in theology, one is liable to forget the other danger to which the refusal to philosophize would have exposed the Christian faith. Christianity would have entered the modern era cut off from science and philosophy, unfit to pursue with them a fruitful dialogue, unable to defend itself if attacked, and unable to benefit the sciences with its own light.

No special effort is required to imagine this situation. By an extraordinary reversal of history, the world of Islam, whose scholars and philosophers had played a decisive part in promoting and fostering the development of scholastic theology, closed its doors to philosophy at the very moment the Christian world was welcoming it. The results are a matter of record, and Ernest Renan has noted them with lucidity in the lecture "Islam and Science," which he gave at the Sorbonne on March 29, 1883. Should anyone wonder what effect Islam has produced on the minds of people, he should compare their intellectual condition before and after the conquest. Nearly all the Latin Fathers are

Africans—Tertullian of Carthage, the Numid Arnobius of Sicca and his pupil Lactantius, Saint Cyprian of Carthage, the African Marius Victorinus, the Berber Saint Augustine, in short, all this glorious vanguard of Latin patristic culture so well studied by Paul Monceaux in his monumental *Literary History of Christian Africa*. What splendid gifts these were from Africa to the Church of Rome while the latter had only the works of Saint Ambrose and of Saint Jerome to put in the balance! The complete intellectual sterilization of these people followed their islamization. Of the much abused scholasticism this at least can be said: it protected the West against this peril. "It is the proper and special office of the scholastic theologians to bind together by the fastest chains human and divine science." Diderot and Voltaire should have remembered that the triumph of scholastic theology in the thirteenth century had made their own existence possible. One does not easily imagine a Voltaire and a Diderot in countries of Islamic culture.

Such as it is ordinarily presented, cut off from the body of the encyclical of which it is the conclusion, the instruction issued by the Pope to restore in schools the way of philosophizing proper to Saint Thomas Aquinas and even his "wisdom," does not make much sense. And, indeed, why this unique privilege? Would not other scholastic philosophies and theologies serve the same purpose? This choice is easily explained in the historical perspective of the encyclical. In the first place, as Leo XIII has carefully demonstrated on the strength of many documents, it was not he who made the choice, it was the Church. His only contribution was to confirm it by bringing together the testimonies of his predecessors and of the Councils in favor of Thomistic theology. The whole thing rests on this point and it is important to grasp its exact meaning. It is that, from the early fourteenth century and ever since, the Church has always recognized herself in the doctrine of Saint Thomas. She knows she always can turn to it with the certainty of finding in it, along with a faithful expression of her own thought, all the treasures of revelation and tradition, organically ordered, interpreted, and clarified by a felicitous use of the natural light of reason.

To elaborate such a doctrine meant simply to bring to its point of perfection the *genus philosophandi,* the "manner of philosophizing" initiated by the Fathers as early as the second century of the Christian era. Far from being directed against anyone, Leo's choice of Thomism was intended as an act of homage toward the whole body of the Christian tradition thus honored in the work of the man who, expressly claiming that tradition as his own, had carried it to its point of perfection. There would be no point in singing once more the praises of Saint Thomas Aquinas. What can be said of him makes sense only for those who, through long habit, have lived in close intimacy with the Angelic Doctor. For such friends praise is superfluous. All could make their own the words that Cajetan wrote with such moving gratefulness—in the Foreword to his Commentary on the *Summa*—on the joys which the assiduous study of Saint Thomas brings to his faithful. As they do not know what we are talking about, the others consider the praises excessive and are annoyed by them. It is only in the twofold perspective of the history of the Church and of personal experience that it is possible to understand the honor conferred upon the doctrine of Saint Thomas and to realize its necessity.

As far as one can judge, Pope Leo XIII's chief aim in

the encyclical was not to impose the use of the formula "Christian philosophy." However, since it appears in the title, it is not unreasonable to think that the formula is related to something in the body of the letter. From the moment the question is asked in these terms, the answer is obvious. By this formula the Pope intended to recommend the use of philosophy made by Saint Thomas in the service of theology in *all* its problems. It matters little whether the truths at stake be accessible to natural reason or escape it; taken in its most comprehensive meaning, Christian philosophy transcends the distinction of scholastic philosophy and scholastic theology. It designates the use the Christian makes of the philosophical reason when, in either one of these two disciplines, he associates religious faith and philosophical reflection.

There is certainly something comical in the ban that some philosophers have issued against such a use of philosophy. Why should we not philosophize as we wish? Some of us choose to philosophize about science, others about art, others still, as did James and Bergson, about moral and religious experience. These ways of philosophizing are all good, useful, and open to Christians. Leo XIII says only that there is a better one. Why should those who profess the Christian faith and its doctrines see themselves excluded from philosophy simply because they prefer to philosophize about what they believe? Scholastics have had no scruples about this. Those who now follow their example have none either. When one of them professes to philosophize in a Christian way after the pattern laid down by Saint Thomas and recommended by the Church, they call him a Thomist. And in some cases he really is. Besides, since this is the name they give him, he can do nothing about it. But he will soon find that he is in a somewhat mixed company. He will have to learn to be as tolerant toward the Thomism of his companions as he wishes them to be toward his own. Above all, having had to don this hat, he will need some time to learn how to wear it.

ON BEING A THOMIST

How does one become a Thomist? At what moment? This is not easy to say. For some reason or other a philosopher begins to read Saint Thomas. If he happens to be allergic to that way of thinking, he drops the book and never picks it up again. But if there exists between him and Saint Thomas some spiritual affinity, he will read and reread it. He will then talk about Thomism, write about it, with no other intention than to help others to dispel their ignorance as he slowly dispels his, but many will want something else. They will want to know, not what Saint Thomas Aquinas thinks, but whether you are a Thomist. The only honest answer to give is that, before proclaiming yourself a Thomist, you ought first to try to find out what the Saint actually thought. To do so is a long undertaking and it is an insult to the Saint's memory to proclaim oneself his disciple without knowing exactly what he said. Such scruples are foreign to the noisiest among his followers. What they want you to do is to say that you are a Thomist. They want you to join the Thomist party. Knowing what some of them call Thomism, and that they do not even suspect there is a problem in knowing what it is, the proposition *I am a Thomist* hardly makes sense. Unfortunately, the contrary proposition has a very definite sense. It would seem that many accept being called Thomists because of their deep reluctance to say that they are not.

He who enters upon this road must be ready for some surprises. The first one is that from this moment on he will be treated by the "Thomists" according to their customary ways, which are not always gentle. Should he be French, he can expect to become the object of particular attentions on the part of integrists whose theological fanaticism is matched by the intolerance so common among Frenchmen. The only Thomist in con-

201

temporary France whose thought was lofty, bold, and creative, capable of meeting the most urgent problems and, so to speak, to stand ever ready before all emergencies, was rewarded for his zeal by the incessant, active, and venomous hostility of unhappy creatures who have little else to put in the service of God than their hatred of their neighbors. True enough, greatness as such is unbearable in their eyes. The disciple is not above the master. Every victim of their injustice will remember that Saint Thomas himself suffered from it.

Another possible surprise for the man who "turns Thomist" is that for the rationalist, that is for the "true philosopher," he will have ceased to exist. This is easily understood. Confronted with the prodigious inflation of books, philosophical journals and conventions prevalent in all civilized countries, it becomes necessary for readers to choose. Now the Thomist is a man who makes it a point to think in philosophy what another man already thought in the thirteenth century. What an excellent pretext to get rid of him! From then on he will find himself honorably classified as belonging among the modern survivors of the "Thomistic school." More simply still, he will find himself labeled a "Neoscholastic," a man neither to be read nor discussed.

Even so, it is not necessary to read many pages from Jacques Maritain to realize that one is dealing with one of the best French writers of our time. He is not always easy to understand and the high quality of his style escapes the readers who do not grasp his thought. But for those who understand him the incessant fecundity of his imagination creates a delightful conspiracy between metaphysics and poetry. His conclusions are annoying? Granted! But why should their own way not to please provoke the hostile silence with which his work is surrounded in his own country? In the *French*

Philosophy Between the Two Wars, published in 1942, Louis Lavelle found nothing to say about Jacques Maritain, except that he criticized Descartes. In a *Survey of French Philosophy,* published in 1946, another philosopher ventured this remark about him: "Others are connected with Thomism, like Jacques Maritain." But how could I forget the twenty-first of March, 1936, the day when this noble mind honored with his presence a meeting of the French Society of Philosophy? He spoke there his usual language. A philosopher who had come from Mars for the occasion would not have been less understood. The excellent Bouglé was the least fanatic among the representatives of secular philosophy. He was most anxious that his Catholic colleagues should feel they were trusted by him, and as a result he strove to prove it to them by courageous decisions. He came out of this meeting visibly preoccupied, even worried. "Say," he whispered in my ear, taking me by the arm in a friendly way, "what is the matter with him? I think he is crazy."

The professed Thomist, then, should not be surprised at the solitude that will surround him. If his own country does not want him, Christendom is vast enough and some countries are generous enough to offer him the public he cannot find at home. Such things have happened. If the synagogue of the "laicists" excludes him, he still will have the opportunity, no doubt without enthusiasm, to turn to the Gentiles. The main thing is that, in a great mind that is also a great heart, such isolation never breeds bitterness. Let his generosity be an example to us. A man may have to live in isolation from his own country and his own time, but he should not let his country and time become foreign to him. On the contrary, the only legitimate reason to call oneself a Thomist is that one feels happy to be one and is anxious

to share this happiness with those who are receptive
to it.

A man becomes aware of being a Thomist on the day
he realizes that from then on he will no longer be able
to live without the company of Saint Thomas Aquinas.
He feels in the *Summa Theologiae* as a fish in the sea;
away from it he feels out of his element, and cannot
wait to go back to it. More deeply, this is what gives
the Thomist the joyous feeling that he is free. Essentially a Thomist is a free mind. His freedom does not
consist in having neither master nor God but rather in
having no master other than God. And indeed God is
for man the only bulwark against the tyrannies of other
men. God alone delivers from fears and timidities a
mind that otherwise would die of starvation in the
midst of plenty. Left to itself, it will be unable to choose
and will therefore die either from starvation or from
indigestion. The happiness of the Thomist is the joy
he experiences in feeling free to welcome all truth from
whichever side it may come. The perfect expression
of this liberty of the Christian man is that of Saint
Augustine: *Dilige et quod vis fac: Love and do what
you will.* In exactly the same spirit and the same deep
sense, but in no other, the disciple of Saint Thomas can
likewise say: *Believe, and think what you will.* Like
charity, faith is a liberator. Incidentally, this is a reason
why the Christian should willingly accept being considered as a rather unusual specimen by non-Christian
thinkers.

After this, the candidate to the office of a Thomist will
be well-inspired to arm himself with patience and, as
an experienced traveler, to be willing to put up with
strange roommates. I shall never forget the unfortunate
professor of philosophy I once met in one of those
countries where the State forces upon the Church,

which cannot help it, the active support of its own policy. I asked him what kind of philosophy he was teaching. He answered: "Thomism, of course." And as I was expressing my pleasure over meeting a fellow Thomist, he answered quite candidly: "No, not at all, I am not a Thomist, but I do not want to lose my job. I have no other choice." I could not blame him. People are past all sense of shame when, decaying together, politics, philosophy, and religion lose their honor at once.

The Church herself is a society. Her citizens too are not always wholly docile, and when her discipline does not suit them, they find ways to get around her laws. Father Pedro Descoqs, S.J., was a zealous upholder of the metaphysics of Suarez, which deeply differs from that of Saint Thomas, especially on the meaning of the first principle, namely, being. When two philosophers do not agree on being, they agree on nothing. It happens that Father Descoqs was a Suarezian. On the other hand, being a Jesuit, he was faithfully subject to the directives of the Holy See; so he was a Thomist. Still, he found a way out of the situation. As he could not turn Suarez into a Thomist, he turned Thomas into a Suarezian. Until his last day, this man who was so intelligent, so excellently informed on the philosophies of the day, this subtle dialectician, at once astute and supple, obstinately upheld this enormity, not indeed that the composition of essence and existence was an error, which would be no more than a debatable philosophical opinion, but rather that *Saint Thomas himself had never taught it!* In support of his opinion, he had an irrefutable argument, as follows. The Common Doctor of the Church could not have taught anything absurd; now the composition of essence and existence was a contradictory and absurd notion; hence the Common Doctor of the Church did not teach it. Those who think that Father Descoqs did not believe the argument himself are completely mistaken. He believed it so fully that, when he saw no way to convince a friend, he preferred to break with him. He sent a parting letter and that was the end of it.

The most commonly accepted way of being a Thomist, and perhaps the only possible one, is to reduce the doctrine of Saint Thomas to what one understands of it. This often means leaving out a great deal, but this sin of omission cannot be completely avoided. Since we are all guilty of it, we should not feel disheartened in seeing others indulge in the same fault. However, there is something upsetting in this experience. Some of us remember reading and teaching the doctrine of Saint Thomas for years without realizing the true meaning of its notion of being, on which, in philosophy, everything else hangs. How long was I able to circle round this notion without seeing it? Twenty years perhaps. Worse still, theologians who have deeply penetrated the meaning of the Thomistic notion of God have been known to teach and to preach the doctrine of Thomas Aquinas without ever suspecting the true meaning of the composition of essence and existence in finite beings. To know that oneself is mistaken on this point would be consoling. For if it is possible in good faith to be so utterly wrong on a doctrine that one knows and loves, to whose spreading he is dedicated and to which he is bound by a double allegiance, the Church and the religious order that he has freely chosen, who can flatter himself that he has really understood it? *If the salt lose its savor, wherewith shall it be salted?*

The safest remedy is to go back to the encyclical *Aeterni Patris* and to the advice that we draw the wisdom of Thomas Aquinas from its very source: *ut sapientia Thomae ex ipsis ejus fontibus hauriatur.* But

206

we are at such a distance from the source that, finding the undertaking very difficult, we call our predecessors to the rescue. This cannot be avoided. That is why, after inviting us to draw from the source, the Pope added: "or at least from those rivulets which, derived from the very fount, have thus far flowed, according to the established agreement of learned men, pure and clear." Unfortunately, water gets muddy pretty near the source. Moreover this agreement among learned men is not so easy to find. Bring together Capreolus, Cajetan, and Bañes and they will soon part company. How to choose? Only by comparing these rivulets with the fountain, a long and complex operation which multiplies the chances of error and whose study usually leads to the conclusion that each interpretation of the doctrine is based on a certain part of the truth seen by the interpreter and mistaken by him for the whole truth. To expect such disagreements will protect the philosopher against intolerant dogmatism or, at the opposite extreme, discouraged skepticism. In the last analysis, everyone will be responsible for his own decisions. Besides, only an uneducated mind (*indisciplinatus*) will expect from his effort more certainty than the nature of the object allows. Let us not be deceived on the point. A reader of Saint Thomas takes no pleasure in parting company with such interpreters of the doctrine as Cajetan or Bañes, men equally famous for acumen and learning. In such cases he cannot fail to see that the odds are against him. Still, since these great men themselves did not always agree, the case is not closed. The justly famous axiom should never be forgotten: *Thomas, his own interpreter.* In other words: Do not judge Saint Thomas by his commentators, judge his commentators (including yourself) by Saint Thomas.

The initiation to Thomism does not end there, for the

work of Saint Thomas is a whole world, indeed, several worlds in one. There is the world of the word of God, Scripture, which is infinite in itself. There is the world of the Fathers, one of whom, Saint Augustine, will suffice for a lifetime of work. There is the world of Aristotle and many other philosophers, whose limits recede when one is about to reach them. Finally, there is the personal world of Saint Thomas himself, at the core of the others, opening new vistas on them all, but so deepseated, so discreet, so anxious to keep in the background whenever possible that there is always a danger of crossing it unawares. There is, however, a sure sign of its presence. It is there when, after listing two, ten, sometimes twenty reasons in favor of a certain conclusion, Saint Thomas writes the word *esse* (to be), a word that belongs to all but of which he makes a very personal use. With him, particularly in metaphysics and theology, it is a light that clears up all difficulties. The light of *esse* should be followed everywhere it shines and sought for when it is hidden from sight; but it should be carefully used, not to dim the other lights, but to purify and intensify them.

Why turn to Saint Thomas rather than to the other Doctors? First, because his teaching does not exclude theirs, but rather includes every one of them so far as they are true. With Saint Thomas one does not give up any truth. Second, because the Church has appointed him her own Common Doctor and prescribes that he be followed wherever, faithful to the proper vocation of wisdom, his teaching coincides with her authentic doctrine. I know that this kind of argument is exasperating for pure rationalists, but Catholics at least cannot possibly disregard it, the more so as the Catholic is not without having his own reasons.

Jesus Christ, twelve apostles soon joined by that extraordinary man of God, Saint Paul, this is the small group from which, about two thousand years ago, came forth the abundant source of Christian doctrine. During these twenty centuries obstacles have not been lacking, but nothing stopped its course. The most dangerous of them were the temptations of reason; the spokesmen of Christian truth never sacrificed faith to it. The history of the Council of Nicaea provides an excellent vantage point from which to appreciate the greatness of the spectacle. Arius was a sensible man, and common sense was on his side. For how can one fail to see that a son cannot be equal to the father from whom he derives his existence? Humanly speaking, the only chance of survival that the Church had was to turn Arian, because that was the way of reason. In fact, the whole civilized world nearly became Arian. It was then that, obstinately siding with the word of God, the Church preferred to trust faith rather than dialectic. This was only one of the first among so many decisive choices, frowned upon by human prudence, when the Church engaged herself fully, at great risk, to remain faithful to the core of truth which it is her mission to preserve and which she never betrays because her knowledge of its secret is infallible. The Church knows that by refusing the temptations of "vain philosophy" she may suffer temporary losses but, by giving in, she would cease to exist.

In history there is no other example of a spiritual society made of men united by their common love of a truth transcending reason which they have kept intact for twenty centuries. One would also look in vain for another example of a religious faith feeding for two thousand years a stream of rational speculation and, in fact, of philosophy, bent upon the task of defining its object, defending it against its enemies from the outside, providing it with arguments, striving to achieve some understanding of mysteries which it yet does not pretend to dispel. This long procession of Doctors of all origins, succeeding one another in the course of centuries, each and every one intent on keeping intact the teaching of a man who, for only three years, preached the doctrine of salvation to poor, simple, and uneducated men: only three years of public life and this wide stream of doctrine fecundating all regions of the earth without allowing any worldly powers to alter its course! Nothing can here replace the direct and personal experience of history. Those to whom leisure has been granted to acquire it know that a more than human force is at work in it. There are some for whom the mere sight of these twenty centuries of doctrinal creativity, unexplainable by mere human interests, is by itself a manifest proof of the existence of a God immediately present to His Church. But perhaps this view of history can be obtained only as the reward of a life devoted to its study.

The faith of the Church is not enough for an understanding of the doctrine of Saint Thomas, but it is necessary. Without faith the literal meaning of the texts may be understood, the deep meaning of a thought entirely devoted to the service of the faith will never be fully understood. In short, the understanding of a Christian philosophy requires from its interpreter a genuinely Christian approach. Hence the failure of most attempts to treat it as a non-Christian philosophy. Here again the philosophy of Aristotle is not at stake. In his commentaries on the writings of the Philosopher, Saint Thomas is not principally concerned with his own philosophy but with Aristotle's. Saint Bonaventure distinguishes between the commentator, who adds to a text only what is necessary to make it understood, and the author, whose chief intention is to express his own thought although he may wish incidentally to quote other writers. Saint Thomas is only a commentator in his writings on Aristotle. For his personal thinking one must look at the two *Summae* and similar writings, in which he shows himself an author in the proper sense of the word. Even in the astonishing tract, *On Being and Essence*, the level of theology is not far from the surface. To neglect the intention of the doctrine is deliberately to expose oneself to missing its meaning.

The most original notions, and the deepest, in the doctrine of Saint Thomas reveal themselves only to him who reads it as a theologian. The very way to read him is thereby modified. From the height of theology the reader will overlook all the parts of philosophy that cannot be put to the service of faith. On the contrary, Thomas will be seen using a variety of philosophical languages irrespective of the meanings they had in the doctrines from which he borrowed them. It is not uncommon to see him supporting one of his conclusions by arguments borrowed from philosophers as different as Aristotle, Avicenna, Boethius, Nemesius, and Saint John Damascene; but the properly Thomistic meaning of the thesis at stake cannot be obtained from these authors themselves. It can be found only in Saint Thomas himself who accepts their arguments as understood in his own doctrine, and as expressive of his own thought.

The Thomist apprentice will then be wary of the philological methods from which so many historians hope to obtain an almost scientific interpretation of the texts. For instance, let us not put too much trust in the quest for sources. No doubt it is necessary to identify quotations and to check their interpretation by the theologian, but this should be the job of the editor of the text; its interpreter undertakes it only if it has not been done by someone else. It is one thing for an author to quote, the way he understands the quotation is another thing. In reading Thomas Aquinas it is often dangerous to understand quotations from Augustine and Boethius, Avicenna and even Aristotle, in the sense the quoted sentences have in the works of these writers. The sense sometimes is their own sense, but it always is that of Saint Thomas. The theologian Thomas Aquinas often is the source of his own sources; he himself, not the Philosopher, uses philosophical notions, judgments, and arguments to achieve some understanding of the Christian faith.

The same remark applies to the "scientific" method held in honor by some historians, which consists in gathering *all* the passages related to a doctrinal position before attempting its interpretation. Preliminary inquiries of this sort are most useful, and they cannot be too extended, but one should not expect miraculous results from this method. On the contrary, it has its own dangers. Two passages of the same author handling what looks like the same problem are only comparable if they consider it from the same point of view and approach it in the same spirit. How many pseudo-evolutions historians have imagined because they have understood as changes in doctrine mere changes in the perspective under which the doctrine visualized certain problems! The difficulty is already present at the level of philosophy, but it is multiplied considerably in the theology of Saint Thomas who, more interested in thought than in language, so frequently conveys his own meaning in languages that are not his. Texts should then not be counted but weighed.

To apply to theological writings the methods of historical inquiry suited to philosophical writings is not entirely safe. To commit errors on the meaning of the master's thought does not disqualify one as a Thomist. Otherwise there would be no Thomists. What is required is not to approach the study of the doctrine in the state of mind of a philosopher who, after reaching the limit of natural theology, imagines that, in order to go further, he has only to sustain *the same effort* on a different ground. The perspective itself should really be inverted; it is the very nature of the effort that should be changed. However far we can go in the footsteps of Aristotle, and even prolonging our explorations of the divine by means of the speculations of Plato, Plotinus, and Proclus, we shall never reach the gate to sacred theology. It is not to be found at the term of metaphysics, nor above metaphysics, but outside it; it is, so to speak, somewhere else. To enter it one should first establish oneself in faith, that is, not merely in the assent of the intellect to a body of propositions held as true because revealed by God, but also in the very same virtue of faith of which it has already been said that it was in us as a participation in God's self-knowledge. In the words of Charles Péguy:

> *Aux quatre cardinales*
> *Vertu formelle.*
> *Aux trois théologales*
> *Grace réelle.*

Grounded in the theological virtue of faith, never to be found without hope and love, the theologian uses all his natural resources to obtain an imperfect and provisory knowledge of the object of faith. Theology thus puts him on his way to the vision of God he hopes to enjoy in the future life. As if swimming upstream toward the source, the intellect of the theologian proceeds, within faith, toward the secret abode where he already dwells, but which he desires to see otherwise than "in part" and "through a glass in a dark manner." None who is not a saint can pretend to go very far along this way, but there is no other one in which to follow the master. Everyone can at least set out on the road and let God decide how far he will be permitted to go. Whatever the outcome, the art of being a Thomist will be acquired and perfected in this undertaking, namely, philosophizing, as only a Christian can, *within* faith.

The Future of Christian Philosophy

The forms Christian philosophy will assume in the coming centuries is the secret of the future. Who in the time of Saint Augustine could have foreseen Saint Thomas Aquinas? The theology of the two Doctors is substantially the same, but the form of the one could not be predicted from that of the other. We can only try to foresee the type of changes of which this kind of philosophy is still susceptible, and even this can be done only on the basis of its past history.

Taking the thirteenth-century theological renovation as typical of such changes, it would seem that they take place when two distinct spiritual forces happen to meet. On the one side there is a relatively sudden scientific advance whose effect is to replace an ancient view of nature by a new one; on the other hand, there is the Christian faith embodied in the Church and defined by tradition. Speaking in general terms, but not inaccurately, one can say that from this contact there is born a third kind of knowledge, distinct from the two preceding ones and yet owing something to both. It is essentially a view of the world inspired by science but put to the service of religion. In such a synthesis everything starts from faith and returns to it. It seems to result from an effort of faith to master all the understanding of itself of which it is capable. A great scientific revolution is for theology an invitation to rejuvenate its formulation by interpreting this new visage of a changing universe in the light of unchanging Christian faith.

There have already been several such encounters, and such a one is taking place in our own day. Contemporary science is transforming the appearance of nature under our very eyes, and theology cannot afford not to take this event into account. In his *Aeterni Patris*, Leo XIII himself has stressed the religious reason that makes it a necessity for theologians to be attentive to the progress of sciences. Since human understanding can rise to the consideration of an intelligible order only from the order of material things, "nothing [is] of greater use to the philosopher than diligently to search into the mysteries of nature and to be earnest and constant in the study of physical things." If there are errors in the previously accepted view of the world, let them be discarded! Never will the Christian philosopher be excused from keeping informed of the new conquests of science. Some will see this attitude as a mere gesture of politeness toward science, or perhaps not even that. They will interpret it as an awkward attempt to look "modern." This is a mistake. The Church is so sure of the truth of faith that she sees in each advance of science the sure promise of a corresponding progress in the intellection of faith, which is the very substance of Christian philosophy. Let us never forget Saint Paul: *Invisibilia Dei* . . . The better we understand nature the better we shall know God.

Leo XIII was not satisfied with defining Christian philosophy. He himself gave conclusive proof that the notion was fruitful. It is strange that so few of our contemporaries, I mean among Catholics, seem to realize that Pope Leo XIII was the greatest Christian philosopher of the nineteenth century and one of the greatest of all time. Moreover, he expressly claimed the responsibility of this high office when, on March 19, 1902, on the occasion of the twenty-fifth anniversary of his election, he looked back on his past and recalled the main acts of his pontificate. He then gave a list of nine of his encyclicals and, remarkably enough, he did not list them according to their chronological order. Nothing was easier for him than to do so and, had he done it, it would today seem that this was the natural thing to do. But the list shows another order, whose reason is obvious:

1. *On Christian Philosophy* (1879): *Aeterni Patris*
2. *On Human Liberty* (1888): *Libertas Praestantissimum*
3. *On Christian Marriage* (1880): *Arcanum Divinae Sapientiae*
4. *On Freemasony* (1884): *Humanum Genus*
5. *On Civil Government* (1881): *Diuturnum*
6. *On the Christian Constitution of States* (1885): *Immortale Dei*
7. *On Socialism* (1878): *Quod Apostolici Muneris*
8. *On the Rights and Duties of Capital and Labor* (1891): *Rerum Novarum*
9. *On Christian Citizenship* (1890): *Sapientiae Christianae*

Taken together and in the order in which the Pope himself has listed them, these nine encyclicals constitute what can be called the *Corpus Leoninum* of Christian philosophy in the nineteenth century. The great subjects treated by Leo XIII and after him by Pius XI and Pius XII were among those that only a pope has authority to handle, but they help us to realize how, while remaining itself, Christian philosophy can renew its teaching. Every Christian philosopher is called upon to imitate this illustrious example in his own modest sphere. To do so he should also know that, in this respect, our situation differs from that of the thirteenth century. For us moderns the writings of Aristotle contain his philosophy, but for Albert the Great, Thomas Aquinas, and the masters of the Parisian Faculty of Arts, what they contained was science. When one of them had finished commentating on Aristotle's encyclopedia, he thought he had learned and taught cosmography, physics, biology, psychology, and the social sciences. As to metaphysics, it represented for them the natural theology which was reasonably acceptable only on the basis of contemporary science. Today no one—

even scholars and especially scientists—would pretend to master the whole of human knowledge. Modern scholastics, then, are under a delusion when they pretend to teach philosophy according to the order prescribed by Aristotle, that is, by going from the sciences to metaphysics. They themselves go from Aristotle's science to what they believe to be his metaphysics, but the sciences have long ceased to be in their hands. In modern classes of philosophy good students in the sciences not infrequently know more about them than their professor ever will. In a time when even the scientist who deals only with science is generally unable to master in its entirety the scientific discipline of his choice, the pretention of being a living scientific encyclopedia is preposterous.

It is to be hoped that, under the pressure of necessity, scientists themselves will spontaneously feel the need to compare the more general results they consider safe and to interpret them, so far as that is possible, to intelligent laymen. This is already being done. We all have been invited to attend a continuous round-table discussion conducted by Einstein, Niels Bohr, Planck, Heisenberg, Louis de Broglie, and others, in which everyone attempted to define in terms of his own contribution to science, fundamental notions such as those of space, time, movement, causality, predictability, and determination, in short, those which Avicenna so aptly called the "generalities of physics": *communia naturalium*. No progress of Christian philosophy is possible as long as those who teach it continue to live in the scientific universe of Aristotle. Not that there is nothing valuable in what is now rightly called the "philosophy of nature," but what is here at stake is chemistry, physics, biology, and astronomy considered precisely as sciences, and it is a fact that the universe of contemporary science is not that of Aristotle.

The future of a Christian philosophy will therefore depend on the existence or absence of theologians equipped with a scientific training, no doubt limited but genuine and, within its own limits, sufficient for them to follow with understanding such lofty dialogues not only in mathematics and physics but also in biology and wherever the knowledge of nature reaches the level of demonstration. One sometimes dreams of a religious order of scientists. But the dream was once true when the most learned men of their own times were called Albert the Great and Thomas Aquinas: both were deeply versed in the sciences, the leading men in philosophy (*praecipui viri in philosophia*), priests, monks, and saints. However, Aristotle should not be disregarded. When the Philosopher defines movement as the act of that which is in potency inasmuch as it is in potency, he is saying nothing that is not true, and what he says is a deep truth. Those who do not understand are the only ones to laugh; only, what he says is not science, it is philosophy. Exactly, it is the metaphysical definition of *becoming*, which is but a mode of being. We should know how to acquire new knowledge without losing the old. This cannot be done unless one is able to handle with competence the language of modern science understood in the sense it now has for scientists. It matters for the future of Christian philosophy that there should always be theologians to understand it, for if they do not take the initiative in incorporating the general conclusions of sciences within the teaching of theology, there will inevitably be Christian men of science to incorporate the teaching of theology within that of positive science. The result is likely to be, as can be seen today, a mixture of science fiction and of mock theology. This is what is called a "modernism." No time is real except the present, and hence modernism is an ever open possibility. Theologians should always be able themselves to retain their initiative and to control new theological developments; thus would be avoided painful crises in which neither religion nor science has anything to gain.

When well-informed theology keeps careful watch, misunderstandings and errors may still happen. They often do, as when two distinct disciplines undertake to collaborate. There are conflicts of jurisdiction and method, as normally arise today between mathematics and physics, or between physicochemistry and biology. No wonder, then, that similar difficulties come up between theology and the scientific disciplines. The thirteenth century was full of conflicts of this type, precisely because it was the golden age of scholastic theology. It is to be expected that we shall see more of the same, but a long experience should at least help to appreciate exactly the nature of such conflicts and the way to settle them.

In this respect, the past teaches that such cases arise when a scientist starts meddling in theology as theology or else when a theologian meddles in science taken precisely *qua* science. The Galileo case is an excellent example of these two errors taking place at one and the same time. Galileo was not disturbed as long as he simply maintained that the earth was revolving around the sun, and not the reverse. The situation deteriorated when he undertook to interpret in his own way the texts of Scripture that seemed opposed to this conclusion. It then became imperative to let him know that Scripture did *not* teach the motion of the earth. Thus far, the theologians were right. In entering the field of biblical exegesis, Galileo had opened himself to criticism; he was minding someone else's business. But when his judges themselves denied the motion of the earth, it was their turn to meddle in astronomy, a science of which Scripture says nothing.

The mathematician and philosopher A. N. Whitehead, coauthor with Bertrand Russell of the *Principia Mathematica,* was a sparkling conversationalist. Besides, he was a priceless friend to have. Wanting to please a Catholic colleague, during the course of one of their long Harvard evenings, Whitehead told him point-blank: "Those judges of Galileo, you know, they were not far wrong! Had they told Galileo only that he had not *demonstrated* the motion of the earth, they would have been three centuries ahead of the science of their time." And, indeed, the earth is certainly not at rest, but it has become difficult to tell with certainty what is revolving around what. Descartes must have been among the first to notice it when, feeling panicky after learning of the condemnation of Galileo, he completely overhauled the mode of exposition of his own physics without meeting with any scientific impossibility. Such disputes are the more vain as, even while they are taking place, the scientific visage of nature never stops changing.

A more recent case is almost comical. While Pasteur was discussing the possibility of spontaneous generation, Catholic philosophers and theologians felt rather disturbed. They feared that Pasteur might reach the conclusion that life can arise from inorganic matter. Pasteur himself was somewhat worried about it, but for the contrary reason. Not as a Catholic, but as a scientist, he did not like the idea that it might look as if his scientific conclusions had been influenced by some secret desire to agree with the traditional teaching of Catholic theology. In fact, the reverse was true. If his conclusions contradicted something, it precisely was the traditional teaching of the scholastics on this point. Saint Thomas and, to the best of my knowledge, all the scholastics who touched this problem, were of the opinion that, from mud heated by the sun, worms, flies and other so-called imperfect animals could be spontaneously generated. Descartes himself was to believe it. True, these are not very big animals, but it is the first living cell that matters. Had Pasteur found only one simple living microbe in a sterilized test tube, the history of modern biology and the history of medicine would not have been what they became in consequence of his conclusions.

Lessons of this sort are sadly useless. Some Christians are today worrying at the thought that sooner or later it will become possible to produce living matter in laboratories experimentally, and perhaps, who knows? some sort of "hominides." Even if this dream should come true, there is nothing in it to disturb us. The only teaching of theology in these matters is that God creates each and every human soul, immediately and individually, every time an embryo becomes the possible body of a man. Whether this embryo is produced naturally or experimentally does not enter the data of the problem. True enough, faith does not demonstrate that each and every human soul is, even now, immediately created by God in the body whose natural development renders it able to receive it. Faith does not prove it, but believes it, and science will never be able to disprove it. The faithful find it hard to reconcile themselves with the idea that, following the words of the Epistle to Timothy, the Lord "inhabiteth light inaccessible." They say this, they believe it, but they forget it when they first need it. The truths of faith are literally *super-*

natural; their objects belong above the order of nature and outside it; and for this very reason they are out of the reach of science. Science has nothing to fear from faith, since scientific truth bears essentially upon nature and is essentially natural knowledge; inversely, the truth of faith is also impregnable in its own domain, for no reason drawn from nature still holds in an order that transcends it by definition. When a theologian inadvertently trespasses on scientific ground, he is twice at fault, for just as he should not expect to hold his theology from natural sciences, so also the scientist is not supposed to draw his physics from theology. This is not the only instance when neighbors get along better by staying at home.

Such quarrels result mainly from usurpations of competence. They are so frequent on the part of science that they are almost the rule. Most scientists are unable to discern with precision the limits of their own science, that is to say, the exact point beyond which demonstrated certitude gives way to the views of imagination. Who could blame them? The illusion is unavoidable. It is even natural, for science would never progress if imagination did not anticipate today the scientific truth of tomorrow. The danger appears at the point where the scientist who follows his reasonable anticipations ascribes to the undemonstrable a probability akin to the certitude of the demonstrated. He does not distinguish between the free play of his imagination creating a world of its own and the insight of the same power of the mind inventing within the boundaries of given reality. Artists imagine what could be, scientists imagine that which is. Wild extrapolation is the pet sin of the wrong kind of imagination in scientific research. Countless instances of that error can be enumerated.

The most remarkable extrapolation of this type, since

the universal mathematicism of Descartes, was seen among the scientists of the nineteenth century who decided that everything in the world obeyed the laws of a universal mechanicism and determinism. To justify this attitude they began by recognizing only quantitative relations among things, which practically amounted to reducing everything to matter. This was a natural step. When he follows his imagination the scientist is naturally inclined to picture to himself the universe such as it has to be in order to be explainable in terms of his own science. This is the natural error so aptly denounced by Aristotle, which consists in conceiving being *qua* being under the form of one of its particular modes. This time, however, normal as it was, the case was somewhat different. The method of physicomathematics itself, quite apart from its concrete applications, was being turned into a universal law of nature. In other words, it was then decreed that what could be known of reality was in itself such as it had to be in order to be scientifically intelligible. Since, they said, the universe is not entirely knowable unless it consists exclusively of quantitative relations ruled by mechanical laws, this was obviously what it really was.

The operation was fantastically arbitrary, but it nonetheless took hold of innumerable minds with the force of a religious faith. This is in effect what it was, but it mistook itself for science and insisted on being considered as such. In our own day Marxism still survives as a belated witness to this illusion. It was the very illusion that Bergson had dispelled in the only way it could be efficaciously done. Inserting the blade of the knife between the articulations of the doctrine, his analysis uncovered a sophism latent in every joint. Had his refutation of universal mechanism been the work of some theologian, what a triumph for Christian philosophy!

It cannot boast of this success, but at least it profited by it. More than one contemporary of the event immediately perceived its significance. Bergson had freed philosophy by demonstrating, through an analysis of universal determinism, that what pretended to be science actually was a very questionable metaphysics. Saint Thomas had already put into practice the precious method of "you have not demonstrated that. . . ." Aristotle did not demonstrate that the world was eternal: he said it was, but he did not really prove it. Averroes did not prove that there was but one intellect for the whole of human kind: he asserted this, but his arguments were not conclusive. And so forth. This critique of the philosophical reason by the reason of the theologian is one of its necessary functions. That is why it is all the more imperative for the theologian that he should first acquire the scientific and philosophical competence without which he could not make his judgments.

Christian men of science are likely to be the ones who will oblige him to exercise his judiciary powers rather often. As Christians they have faith; as scientists they have learning; and the slowness of theology to move forward, however understandable it may be, has nonetheless this consequence, that it annoys generous hearts anxious to serve. Besides, the really dangerous persons are less real scientists than Christians with a smattering of science. On the strength of scientific interests respectable in themselves, convinced that official theology is deplorably lagging behind in matters of science, they feel invested with the personal mission to bring sacred science up to date and, by so doing, to ensure its survival. These reformers sometimes do not have even a smattering of science. I remember one of them, a priest who lived in constant anxiety because of the peril the Church was undergoing for not rallying more openly to the scientific doctrine of evolution. He had a new theology in mind. Asked what sciences he had studied, he answered in all simplicity: "None, but the British encyclopedia has a very good article on the question." I read the article. It was very good indeed. Still it was not enough.

Men of this type are generally excellent. As often as not they are apostles at heart, but it must be said that, although they are priests, they entertain rather hazy notions about theology. Still less are they clearly aware of the place they occupy in a tradition they have inherited and which, while it does not deprive them of their free initiative, nevertheless conditions their intellectual activity. The future of Christian philosophy is necessarily dependent on its past and we come too late to change its style. Pope Leo XIII has rightly said that the philosophical venture began as early as the time of Saint Justin and that it continued for more than twelve centuries without changing its rule. Disorder finally crept into it. At the time of the encyclical it had reached such proportions that, spreading from the men to societies, it threatened them with ruin. One cannot overemphasize the fact that, in the mind of the Pope, the origin of *Aeterni Patris* was his anguish over so many wars or revolutions and his ardent desire to remove their cause. Now the prime source is the disorder in the minds of men which results when those who cast off the Catholic faith profess to follow no other guide than the philosophical reason. An abnormal multiplication of philosophical systems, whose end is not in sight, has always attended this disorder. The necessary condition to insure the future of Christian philosophy is to maintain the primacy of the word of God, *even in philosophical inquiry*. I am tempted to say, *above all* in matters of philosophical speculation. In order to bring about this result, we must will it. Here, however, even though Christian, the philosopher has exhausted his resources. It is not in him to change hearts. If we knew the gift of God, if we understood that the Church and Jesus Christ are one, there would be no hearts to change.

Were this point understood, many ill-advised undertakings would be avoided. Their incentive is the taste for innovation that so curiously blends with that for imitation. What is here at stake, then, is not the personal gift of invention, which true scientists and philosophers possess but for which they do not care; but rather the inordinate passion for conformism that perpetually sets minds on the track of novelty as such. *Hoc novitatis studium, cum homines imitatione trahantur:* such is the root of the evil, and since Catholic philosophers are men, some of them have yielded to the temptation. At this point the language of the Pope is so full of meaning that commentaries would weaken it: ". . . throwing aside the patrimony of ancient wisdom, [they] chose rather to build up a new edifice than to strengthen and complete the old by aid of the new—ill-advisedly, in sooth, and not without detriment to the sciences. For, a multiform system of this kind, which depends on the authority and choice of any professor, has a foundation open to change, and consequently gives us a philosophy not firm, and stable, and robust like that of old, but tottering and feeble." And let us not forget the warning contained in the conclusion: "And if, perchance, it sometimes finds itself scarcely equal to sustain the shock of its foes, it should recognize that the cause and the blame lie in itself." For Christian philosophy the sources of unity are Scripture and tradition.

One of the chief evils opposed by the Church at the time of the modernist crisis was the rejection of this twofold authority. Those who today have to reproach themselves with their hesitations at the time, their reservations, their sullen assent to the magisterial authority of the Church, have since had to learn that the Church is always right. Many tormented faces of Christians, even of priests, still haunt the memory of those who lived during those years of spiritual confusion; and yet most of the problems that then seemed tragic have ceased to exist. Some of them gave up the priesthood to answer the call of what they considered their duty as scholars or scientists; their lives are now nearing their term or have already reached it. What brilliant use did they make of their freedom?

Alfred Loisy, an exegete of great learning, ended his life, if not in failure, at least in melancholy isolation. The slightest kindness found him responsive. When a younger colleague called to inform him of a possible academic honor, Loisy answered gently: "Yes, I know. You will be elected. And then, later on, you will be made a member of the Institute. It is only natural." After a short silence he continued: "Now be careful. Do not be a candidate in winter time, because there are visits to make. Consider Batiffol; he made this mistake." Then with a kind of secret amusement: "And he died!" Remembering that there was no love lost between the two men the visitor hastened to change the conversation. He broached the subject of Loisy's current writing, but it seemed that there too things were not going very well. Writing books is not the end of it, Loisy observed; "they have to be published and I can publish a new book only on the revenue left by the preceding one." As he was answered in all sincerity that this was no problem, Loisy continued: "Make no mistake, my books do not sell well. Catholics do not read them, of course. Protestants are few and not much more interested. As to those of our colleagues who practice historical criticism, they look upon me as a timid mind long since left behind. No indeed, there is no one standing with me." The visitor could only retire discreetly. But he was to remember these words in hearing another historian, Charles Guignebert, complain of the unfriendly attitude of a younger biblical exegete toward him. "It is amazing," Guignebert said candidly, for he was basically a good man, "they treat me like dirt." Like Saturn, critical exegesis devours its own children.

Scientific exegesis so-called, then, did not have the feeling of going from triumph to triumph. Those who gambled their lives on this card lost it. Some of them finally became aware of their failure, but a long time after everyone around them did. An excellent Protestant minister said that much toward 1922 while welcoming a new colleague at the École Pratique des Hautes Études Religieuses in Paris: "Those people are out on a limb and they are sawing it off." He was interested in the question. For if, by an impossibility, you could take Scripture away from a Catholic, he would still have the Church, but should the same thing happen to a Protestant, he would have nothing left. In point of truth Loisy was not right, but some of his Catholic critics could have done better than to maintain against him, on certain secondary points, illusions of perspective that they mistook for truth. Entirely right at the time were those who, in total submission to the Church, all the more courageously carried on the quest for truth, meaning thereby that most rare of realities, a *scientifically demonstrated* conclusion. Were he still with us, Father Lagrange could view with satisfaction the fruit of his twofold fidelity to science and the Church. He was the one to be right.

One can think of no clearer example of a truly Christian attitude. Just as Christian exegesis can improve, so can Christian philosophy, but only through an increased fidelity to the teaching of revelation held in trust by the Church and to the progress of scientific knowledge. What a Catholic can learn from life, if he devotes it to these studies, is simply that between these two lights there is a difference of order and authority, a literally "hierarchical" difference. Science and philosophy can help Christian philosophy to constitute itself as a science, but neither one nor the other will add anything to the truth of the faith that engages their services. The perishable parts of a theology are precisely those it had to borrow from the science of its time. The same remark applies to philosophy. All metaphysics become outdated because of their physics: that of Saint Thomas (and of Aristotle himself) because the Aristotelian physics became obsolete, that of Descartes because of the Cartesian mechanics, that of Kant because of the Newtonian physics, and that of the last born, Bergson, who lived just long enough to realize that he could not catch up with the physics of relativity.

One cannot commend the zeal of those who, to promote the progress of Christian philosophy, think it their duty to tie its future to each new scientific view of the world. The source of its own vitality is not found in the advances of science, because it does not hold its truth from science. Christian philosophy observes with warm sympathy the birth of new scientific theories; it wishes them well, it warns them against possible perils, but it never embarks on any one of these ventures. Some apologists always seem afraid to miss the last boat, but there is no last boat. From the stern of your boat you always can see three or four others ready to sail.

Christian philosophy is a history that unfolds from an immutable starting point situated out of time and therefore without a history. It is the unfolding of a progress from a truth itself not susceptible of progress. This truth shares in the nature of God Himself, Who does not change, but the universe on which it sheds its light is subject to continuous change. The worlds of scientific, moral, social, economic, and political invention, even that of artistic creation, are as many continually renewed contributions to which Christian wisdom should lend the warmest attention, to purify them and reveal their affinities with saving truth. It is not the light of Christian truth that changes; on the contrary, it is necessary that it should not itself change so that, perpetually present to the world and faithful to itself, it remains an ever active ferment of progress.

The place of pride attributed to Saint Thomas by the Church appears to many of our contemporaries, even among Catholics, out of proportion, unjustifiable, absurd. One could quote many indignant protests on this point. Some are hardly believable, coming as they do from priests and religious. Why reopen old wounds or inflict new ones? Rather, let every one of those who claim Saint Thomas for their master speak for himself and relate his personal experience without involving others.

In this spirit, I shall say that after a long life spent in the study of Christian philosophy, aware of the evolution it has undergone and which Pope Leo XIII has so aptly described in *Aeterni Patris,* I feel no less deeply impressed by its miraculous fidelity to Christian faith. This is what justifies in my mind the hard obstinacy of the Church in matters of orthodoxy. Without this rigorous watchfulness, always on the lookout for doctrinal deviations, actual or possible, the miracle would soon have come to an end. In this perspective, the choice of a doctrinal norm was a necessity. It is not enough to warn minds against error if one cannot at the same time show them where truth lies. Moreover there are weighty reasons why this doctrinal norm should be the doctrine of Saint Thomas. Speaking as a Christian philosopher and in the perspective of Christian philosophy, I would see the chief reason for it in its conception of the first principles. The metaphysics of Saint Thomas Aquinas is based on a conception of these principles that, while agreeing with the literal meaning of Scripture, at the same time assigns to metaphysics the deepest interpretation of the notion of being ever offered by any philosophy. I call this interpretation of the first principle the deepest of all because, in its light, I can continue to hold as true whatever truth there is in any other philosophy, without any exception, while, at the same time, I receive from it truths on God, nature, and man that only this philosophy can give. Should it be objected that I cannot pretend to stop at Saint Thomas Aquinas the course of the history of metaphysics, and that the time to find something else has come, I would answer that I have neither the authority nor the power to do any such thing. I am simply saying what I think. On the strength of my own experience, I say only that, had I found something more intelligent and true than what Saint Thomas has said about being, I would have been only too pleased to share it with my contemporaries. On the contrary, having reached the conclusion that his metaphysics was deep, fruitful, in short, true, I must content myself with bringing to them this unoriginal conclusion. I am very far from ignoring their efforts, and farther still from minimizing them. I only wish they knew the truth of which I am speaking as well as I know what they consider their own truth. From where I now stand I can see looming in the distance some new philosophies still groping for their forms and I know that I shall have neither the time nor the strength to follow them to their point of perfection. I regret it, but when I see behind me six centuries of speculation during which philosophy has not even been able to keep intact the truth it had inherited, I see no reason to cast it aside if I do not have any hope of finding a better one.

Shall I say, then, that no philosophical progress is still open to Christian philosophy? Scarcely. I think, rather, that Christian philosophy has before itself a future of unending progress provided, precisely, that it remains faithful to the truth of its principles. Every discovery made in any order of knowledge will provide it with an occasion to manifest its fecundity as a supreme wisdom; every progress whatever can be for it an occasion of progress. And what about the principles themselves? Is there no possibility for the further deepening of the notion of being? I do not know. Did I see one, I would proclaim it. No Christian philosopher could have guessed, at the time of Saint Augustine, that it was possible to go farther along the same road. But Saint Thomas was to show that it was possible. God alone knows if a new discovery of the same type remains possible and if, in the course of time, it will take place. We know only that, if it truly takes place, the Church will know it.

Speaking more and more according to my own light, and merely as a witness, I beg only to add that my inability to think of a better metaphysics than that of Saint Thomas is not my ultimate ground for assenting to it. A long reflection on its truth makes me see it as a light capable of absorbing every other light. The Thomistic notion of *esse* (to be) is ultimate in virtue of its very nature. It is the *ultima Thule* of all metaphysics; it lays the foundation of metaphysical knowledge for all time. I would hesitate thus to challenge the gospel of progress did I not see on the contrary how little convincing it is. We all know that the ultimate steps of progress are by far the most difficult to achieve. Is it not natural that in the supreme science, which is metaphysics, wherein the intellect comes to grips with the loftiest objects of knowledge, progress become proportionally rare and arduous? It even seems evident that the more deeply such progress takes us within the core of its object, the more improbable a further advance becomes. Far from finding unreasonable my absolute certainty that this Christian metaphysics is true, my continuous study of it confirms my belief in its perenniality.

Who would believe that this noble ship, which for so many centuries has carried her load without ever departing from her course, is today about to alter it or to reach its term? The force that launched her is not spent, nor will she lack the assistance of Him Who promised to be with her to the end of time. We passengers may sometimes forget who we are and whither we want to go. We resemble the man "beholding his own countenance in a glass," of whom Saint James says that "he beheld himself, and went his way, and presently forgot what manner of man he was." And yet the course to follow is safe if the pilots do not lose sight of the "friendly star"—*sidus amicum*—which through the ages remains the infallible guide of Christian philosophy, faith, the mother of hope and the beginning of the life of blessedness.

ABOUT THE AUTHOR

Born in Paris in 1884, ETIENNE GILSON was graduated from the University of Paris in 1907 and took his doctorate at the Sorbonne in 1913. While serving in the French army in World War I, he was captured at the Battle of Verdun, and spent his years of captivity (1915–18) studying, among other things, the philosophy of St. Bonaventure and the Russian language. In 1919 he was appointed professor at the University of Strasbourg, and in 1921 he became Professor of History of Philosophy at the Sorbonne, where he had studied with Lucien Lévy-Bruhl and Victor Delbos. During the next years he achieved world-wide acclaim as a medievalist and a writer and regularly visited American and Canadian universities—among them Harvard, Columbia, Virginia and Indiana. In 1932 he inaugurated the first Chair of History of Medieval Philosophy at the Collège de France.

Professor Gilson has held the Gifford lectureship in Aberdeen (1930–31), the William James at Harvard (1938) and the A. W. Mellon Lecture in Fine Arts at the National Art Gallery in Washington, D.C., (1955). During those years he contributed to the creation and direction of the Pontifical Institute of Mediaeval Studies at the University of Toronto, where he is still active. A fellow of the Académie Française since 1947, Etienne Gilson has taken an active part in the political life of France: as a technical adviser at the San Francisco Conference in 1945, a member of the French delegation to UNESCO, as a Senator in 1947, and as a member of the French delegation to the European Convention at La Haye in 1948.

Professor Gilson has written over thirty-five books, including major studies on outstanding theologians and philosophers from St. Augustine to Ockham. Among his recent books are *The Christian Philosophy of St. Thomas Aquinas, The History of Christian Philosophy in the Middle Ages,* and *The Christian Philosophy of Saint Augustine.*